Eat *for*

EXTRAORDINARY

Health

COOKBOOK

Eat *for* EXTRAORDINARY Health COOKBOOK

80+ DELICIOUS RECIPES TO RENEW AND RESTORE

RODALE

© 2016 by Rodale Inc.

Photographs © 2016 by Rodale Inc., except pages 4 and 7

Printed in the United States of America
Rodale Inc. makes every effort to use acid-free ∞, recycled paper ♻.

Cover photos (*clockwise from top left*): Scrambled Eggs and Tomato-Turmeric Sauté (*page 2*); Fiesta Turkey Soup (*page 30*); Portobello "Philly" Sandwich (*page 23*); and Cantaloupe with Honey-Spiced Yogurt (*page 124*)

Photographs by Mitch Mandel / Rodale Images, except page 4 by Con Poulos and page 7 by John Kernick
Book design by Joanna Williams

Library of Congress Cataloging-in-Publication Data is on file with the publisher.

ISBN 978-1-62336-796-1   direct mail paperback

2 4 6 8 10 9 7 5 3   direct mail paperback

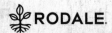

We inspire and enable people to improve their lives and the world around them.
rodalestore.com

contents

introduction

Now that you've read about the incredible powers of the superfoods in *Eat for Extraordinary Health and Healing*, it's time to head to the kitchen and enjoy cooking with these curing ingredients. The recipes found here are loaded with nutrient-dense foods prepared in simple yet delicious ways.

Highlighting plant-based foods, fish, and seafood, along with a higher intake of healthy fats, these recipes are bursting with flavors from fruits like lemons and limes, herbs like basil and cilantro, and spices including black pepper. Salmon, pomegranate, lentils, avocados, and even chocolate are just a few of the tasty ingredients that go into each of these recipes, all available in your grocery store.

Plenty of favorite dishes are included with simple tweaks to boost nutrients. Your family will delight in Tuna Noodle Casserole on page 77, Baked Macaroni and Cheese on page 84, or a simple marinated flank steak on page 56. Check out a new take on a Philadelphia cheese steak with our Portobello "Philly" Sandwich on page 23; it's made with meaty portobello mushrooms in place of the beef and is so satisfying. Vibrant, healing spices such as turmeric and curry liven up any dish like Scrambled Eggs over Tomato-Turmeric Sauté on page 2 or Curried Lentil Soup on page 29.

And let's not forget dessert. Treats like Double Dark Chocolate Pudding on page 134 and the Lemon–Poppy Seed Loaf on page 137 will make you feel like you're indulging, rather than helping to heal. Each recipe is a stepping-stone on the path to a healthier life. It's time to start feeling extraordinary!

breakfast

scrambled eggs and tomato-turmeric sauté

prep time: 10 minutes • **total time:** 25 minutes

2 tablespoons extra-virgin olive oil, divided

4 scallions, sliced diagonally

1 clove garlic, minced

1 tablespoon turmeric

1 pint (12 ounces) red cherry tomatoes

1 pint (12 ounces) yellow cherry tomatoes

½ teaspoon sea salt, divided

8 eggs

¼ teaspoon pepper

2 tablespoons crumbled feta cheese

Toasted whole grain baguette slices

1. Heat 1 tablespoon of the oil in a large skillet over medium-low heat. Cook the scallions, garlic, and turmeric, stirring, for 1 minute. Stir in the tomatoes and cook for 5 minutes, stirring occasionally, or until the tomatoes soften. Sprinkle with ¼ teaspoon of the salt and keep warm.

2. Meanwhile, in a medium bowl, whisk together the eggs, pepper, and the remaining ¼ teaspoon salt. Heat the remaining 1 tablespoon oil in a large skillet over medium heat. Cook the egg mixture for 4 minutes, stirring occasionally, or until set.

3. Divide the eggs and the tomato mixture among 4 plates. Sprinkle with the feta. Serve with the toast.

makes 4 servings

per serving: 259 calories, 15 g protein, 9 g carbohydrates, 18 g fat, 5 g saturated fat, 2 g fiber, 418 mg sodium

italian-style eggs

prep time: 10 minutes • **total time:** 25 minutes

1. Heat a large nonstick skillet over medium-high heat. Brush 1 side of each bread slice with some of the oil. Place the bread slices, oil side down, in the pan. Brush the tops with oil. Cook for about 2 minutes on each side, or until toasted. Place a slice of toast on each of 4 plates or individual baking dishes. Set aside.

2. Return the pan to medium heat. Stir in the remaining oil, the onion, and the bell pepper. Cook, stirring, for 2 minutes, or until the vegetables are softened. Stir in the tomatoes, salt, and pepper. Bring to a boil. Reduce the heat to medium-low and cook for 5 minutes, or until the tomatoes make a chunky sauce. With a large spoon, create 4 indentations in the sauce.

3. Break the eggs, 1 at a time, into a custard cup. Gently tip the egg into 1 of the indentations in the sauce. Repeat with the remaining eggs. Cover and simmer for 6 to 8 minutes, or until the whites are completely set.

4. Use a large spoon to lift each egg and accompanying sauce onto each plate, either next to or on top of the toast. Spoon any remaining sauce evenly around the egg.

makes 4 servings

- 4 slices (½" thick) whole grain French or Italian bread (about 4 ounces)
- ¼ cup extra-virgin olive oil
- 1 small onion, finely chopped
- ½ cup finely chopped green bell pepper
- 6 plum tomatoes, chopped
- ⅛ teaspoon salt
- ⅛ teaspoon pepper
- 4 large eggs

per serving: 310 calories, 11 g protein, 23 g carbohydrates, 20 g fat, 3 g saturated fat, 2 g fiber, 352 mg sodium

blueberry pancakes

prep time: 10 minutes • **total time:** 15 minutes

1½ cups whole wheat
    pastry flour

½ cup ground golden
    flaxseeds

2 tablespoons baking
    powder

½ teaspoon salt

2 large eggs

1½ cups milk, such as soy,
    hemp, almond, rice, or
    dairy

2 tablespoons coconut oil,
    melted, plus more for the
    griddle

4 tablespoons honey,
    divided

2 cups blueberries, divided

1. In a large bowl, combine the flour, flaxseeds, baking powder, and salt.

2. In a medium bowl, beat the eggs. Beat in the milk, oil, and 2 tablespoons of the honey. Mix gently into the flour mixture, then fold in 1½ cups of the blueberries.

3. Preheat a griddle and brush it lightly with oil. Ladle the batter by ¼ cups onto the griddle and cook on both sides until golden brown. Repeat with the remaining batter.

4. Divide the pancakes among 8 plates. Top with the remaining ½ cup blueberries and 2 tablespoons honey.

makes 8 servings

per serving: 256 calories, 7 g protein, 36 g carbohydrates, 9 g fat, 4 g saturated fat, 5 g fiber, 510 mg sodium

wheat-flax crepes with fresh fruit

prep time: 10 minutes • **total time:** 40 minutes

1½ cups 2% milk

2 eggs

¾ cup whole wheat flour

¼ cup ground golden flaxseeds

1 tablespoon honey

2 tablespoons extra virgin olive oil, divided

¼ teaspoon sea salt

1 package (6 ounces) fresh blackberries

1 package (6 ounces) fresh blueberries

½ pint (1 cup) fresh raspberries

1 cup 2% plain Greek yogurt

3 tablespoons honey

1. In a large jar with a tight-fitting lid, combine the milk and eggs. Seal and shake well to combine. Add the flour, flaxseeds, honey, 1 tablespoon of the oil, and the salt. Seal and shake for 1 minute, or until well combined. Let rest for 15 minutes (see Note).

2. Meanwhile, in a medium bowl, combine the berries. Set aside.

3. Heat 1 teaspoon of the remaining oil in an 8" non-stick skillet over medium heat. Pour ¼ cup of the batter into the skillet, swirling to completely cover the bottom. Cook for 1 minute, or until golden brown. Loosen the edge of the crepe with a rubber spatula and carefully flip the crepe over. Cook for 45 seconds, or until lightly golden. Transfer to a plate and repeat using the remaining oil, when needed, and batter to make 8 crepes.

4. Spread 2 tablespoons of the yogurt in the center of each crepe. Evenly top with the fruit. Fold over the sides toward the middle to seal the crepes. Drizzle with the honey.

makes 4 servings

note: It's important to allow the batter to rest, because during this time starch molecules in the flour will absorb any liquid in the batter. This gives it a thicker consistency. Air bubbles will dissipate, and the gluten formed during the mixing will relax, ensuring a thin, uniform structure to the crepes.

per serving (2 crepes): 408 calories, 17 g protein, 56 g carbohydrates, 15 g fat, 3 g saturated fat, 10 g fiber, 198 mg sodium

buckwheat and bran muffins

prep time: 10 minutes • **total time:** 30 minutes

1. Preheat the oven to 350°F. Coat a 12-cup muffin pan with cooking spray.

2. In a medium bowl, stir together the wheat flour, buckwheat flour, bran, flaxseeds, baking powder, baking soda, cinnamon, and salt. In a large bowl, whisk together the milk, eggs, oil, honey, and apple until combined.

3. Add the flour mixture and raisins to the milk mixture, stirring just until combined. Do not overmix. Evenly divide the batter into the muffin cups.

4. Bake for 18 to 20 minutes, or until the tops spring back when lightly pressed and a toothpick inserted in the center comes out clean.

makes 12 servings

tip: These muffins can be frozen, wrapped airtight, for up to 2 months.

¾ cup white whole wheat flour

¾ cup buckwheat flour

¾ cup wheat bran

¼ cup ground flaxseeds

1 teaspoon baking powder

1 teaspoon baking soda

1 teaspoon ground cinnamon

¼ teaspoon salt

1 cup milk, such as soy, hemp, almond, rice, or dairy

2 eggs

3 tablespoons melted coconut oil

½ cup honey

1 small apple, shredded

¾ cup raisins

per serving: 197 calories, 4 g protein, 34 g carbohydrates, 6 g fat, 1 g saturated fat, 3 g fiber, 219 mg sodium

almond-apricot scones

prep time: 20 minutes • **total time:** 40 minutes

1. Preheat the oven to 375°F. Line a baking sheet with parchment paper. Sprinkle a cutting board or surface with 2 tablespoons of the flour.

2. In a large bowl, whisk together the almond meal, ¾ cup flour, granulated sugar, baking powder, ginger, and salt. Grate the butter on the large holes of a box grater and add to the bowl. Stir to combine. Stir in the apricots.

3. In a measuring cup, whisk together the milk, honey, vanilla, and 1 egg. Add to the almond meal mixture and stir until just combined. Transfer to the floured surface and form into a thick disk. Roll into an 8" circle, about ¾" thick, sprinkling flour over the dough and board as needed. Cut into 8 wedges.

4. In a small bowl, whisk together the remaining egg and the water. Lightly brush over the dough. Sprinkle with the raw sugar and almonds, pressing lightly to adhere. Transfer the scones to the prepared baking sheet. Bake for 15 minutes, or until golden brown and a toothpick inserted in the center comes out clean. Cool on the baking sheet for 5 minutes and serve, or transfer to a rack and cool completely.

makes 8 servings

2 tablespoons plus ¾ cup white whole wheat flour

1½ cups almond meal

1 tablespoon plus 1 teaspoon granulated sugar

2 teaspoons baking powder

1 teaspoon ground ginger

½ teaspoon salt

3 tablespoons butter, frozen

1 cup dried apricots, chopped

¼ cup milk, such as soy, hemp, almond, rice, or dairy

3 tablespoons honey

1 teaspoon vanilla extract

2 eggs

1 tablespoon water

2 teaspoons raw sugar

2 tablespoons sliced almonds, toasted

per serving: 307 calories, 9 g protein, 35 g carbohydrates, 17 g fat, 4 g saturated fat, 5 g fiber, 199 mg sodium

papaya-pomegranate yogurt parfait

prep time: 5 minutes • **total time:** 5 minutes

1 teaspoon chia seeds

1 container (6 ounces) vanilla yogurt

3 tablespoons rolled oats

3 tablespoons sunflower seeds

⅔ cup diced papaya

2 tablespoons pomegranate seeds or fresh raspberries

1. Stir the chia seeds into the yogurt in the container and set aside.

2. In a small skillet over medium heat, toast the oats and sunflower seeds for 2 minutes, stirring frequently, or until golden and fragrant. Layer the papaya and pomegranate, yogurt, and oat mixture into a parfait glass or bowl.

makes 1 serving

healthy know-how

If you're purchasing a whole papaya, choosing the perfect one can be challenging. To pick the best papaya with the most flavor, choose one that yields to gentle pressure and has spotty coloring.

per serving: 431 calories, 18 g protein, 51 g carbohydrates, 18 g fat, 3 g saturated fat, 7 g fiber, 123 mg sodium

fruit bowls with ricotta cream

prep time: 20 minutes • **total time:** 20 minutes

1. In a food processor or blender, puree the ricotta and honey until smooth. Place in a medium bowl. Stir in the yogurt and lime zest.

2. In a large bowl, combine the peaches, raspberries, mango, banana, and lime juice. Divide the fruit, ricotta cream, and almonds among 4 bowls.

makes 4 servings

- ½ cup part-skim ricotta cheese
- 1 tablespoon honey
- ¾ cup 0% plain Greek yogurt
- ½ teaspoon grated lime zest
- 2 peaches, sliced
- 1 cup raspberries
- 1 mango, cut into chunks
- 1 large banana, sliced
- 1 tablespoon fresh lime juice
- 2 tablespoons almonds, toasted and coarsely chopped

per serving: 228 calories, 10 g protein, 40 g carbohydrates, 5 g fat, 2 g saturated fat, 6 g fiber, 60 mg sodium

creamy steel-cut oats
with cranberries and pistachios

prep time: 10 minutes • **total time:** 25 minutes

4 cups milk, such as soy, hemp, almond, rice, or dairy

1 cup steel-cut oats

½ teaspoon ground cinnamon

½ teaspoon ground ginger

¼ teaspoon salt

½ cup dried cranberries, chopped

6 tablespoons chopped shelled pistachios

2 tablespoons plus 2 teaspoons maple syrup

1. In a medium saucepan over medium-high heat, bring the milk to a simmer, stirring occasionally to keep the milk from sticking to the bottom of the pan, about 10 minutes. Add the oats, cinnamon, ginger, and salt. Return to a simmer, reduce the heat to medium-low, and cook for 4 minute, stirring constantly, or until thickened.

2. Evenly divide the oats, cranberries, pistachios, and maple syrup into 4 bowls.

makes 4 servings

per serving: 402 calories, 17 g protein, 62 g carbohydrates, 13 g fat, 4 g saturated fat, 6 g fiber, 117 mg sodium

cocoa-cherry smoothie

prep time: 10 minutes • **total time:** 10 minutes

¾ cup frozen dark
   unsweetened cherries

¾ cup milk, such as soy,
   hemp, almond, rice, or
   dairy

¾ cup ice cubes

2 tablespoons unsweetened
   cocoa powder

2 teaspoons ground
   flaxseeds

1 tablespoon honey

½ teaspoon vanilla

In a blender, combine the cherries, milk, ice, cocoa, flaxseeds, honey, and vanilla. Blend for 1 to 2 minutes, or until smooth.

makes 1 serving

healthy know-how

Although highly nutritious, flaxseed also has a high fat content, which can cause them to get rancid. Make sure to store it in the fridge or freezer for no more than 6 months to get the most out of your flaxseed.

per serving: 272 calories, 10 g protein, 49 g carbohydrates, 7 g fat, 2 g saturated fat, 8 g fiber, 105 mg sodium

nut butter–banana smoothie

prep time: 10 minutes • **total time:** 10 minutes

In a blender, process the oats until ground. Add the banana, milk, ice, nut butter, honey, and cinnamon. Blend for 1 to 2 minutes, or until smooth.

makes 1 serving

¼ cup rolled oats

1 medium ripe banana, cut into 1" chunks

¾ cup milk, such as soy, hemp, almond, rice, or dairy

1 cup ice cubes

2 tablespoons almond or cashew butter

2 teaspoons honey

⅛ teaspoon ground cinnamon

healthy know-how

If you don't want a banana smoothie every day but are afraid of your bananas going bad, delay the ripening by storing them in the refrigerator. The skin will turn black, but the banana won't ripen any further.

per serving: 519 calories, 17 g protein, 70 g carbohydrates, 22 g fat, 3 g saturated fat, 10 g fiber, 173 mg sodium

sandwiches, salads, and soups

tuna club

prep time: 15 minutes • **total time:** 20 minutes

2 cans (5 ounces each) tonno tuna in olive oil

2 tablespoons lemon juice

1 heaping teaspoon chopped fresh thyme

1 teaspoon Dijon mustard

¼ teaspoon pepper

2 tablespoons grated red onion

1 tablespoon capers, drained and chopped (optional)

1 loaf whole wheat baguette (about 16")

2 cups firmly packed watercress

½ small English cucumber, thinly sliced

1. Open 1 can of the tuna and drain the oil (about 3 tablespoons) into a small bowl. Add the lemon juice, thyme, mustard, and pepper to the oil and whisk until blended.

2. Open the remaining tuna can and drain, discarding the oil. Add the tuna from both cans to the bowl, mashing with a fork to break the tuna into small pieces. Stir in the onion and capers, if using. Gently toss to blend well.

3. Hollow out the center of the baguette, reserving the center pieces for another use. Spread the watercress along the bottom half of the bread. Top with the tuna salad. Place the cucumber slices on top. Cover with the top half of the bread and cut into 4 pieces.

makes 4 servings

tip: Several different types of tuna are found in canned tuna, including tongol, yellowfin, and albacore. Yellowfin is generally considered the highest quality, with its darker, meatier flavor. Yellowfin is also high in omega-3 fatty acids and vitamin D. Cans labeled "tonna tuna" are usually yellowfin. The other decisions one has in selecting tuna are how it's packed: in oil or water, and solid tuna versus broken pieces. Tuna packed in olive oil often has more flavor and moisture than tuna packed in water.

per serving: 216 calories, 23 g protein, 16 g carbohydrates, 6 g fat, 1 g saturated fat, 1 g fiber, 441 mg sodium

tofu, lettuce, tomato, and avocado sandwich

prep time: 15 minutes • total time: 20 minutes

1. Coat a grill pan with some of the oil.

2. In a small bowl, combine the remaining oil, chili sauce, and soy sauce.

3. In a separate small bowl, combine the mayonnaise and 1 tablespoon of the soy mixture. Heat the pan over medium-high heat.

4. Cook the tofu slices in the grill pan for 2 minutes, or until the tofu is lightly brown. Turn and brush the tops with the remaining soy mixture. Cook for 2 minutes, or until the tofu is golden brown.

5. To assemble the sandwiches, brush the hamburger bun bottoms with the mayonnaise mixture. Top each with a lettuce leaf and a tomato slice. Place 2 slices of tofu on top of each tomato. Top with the avocado slices and the bun tops.

makes 4 servings

1 tablespoon extra-virgin olive oil plus more for coating the pan

2 tablespoons jarred Asian chili-garlic sauce

2 teaspoons reduced-sodium soy sauce

¼ cup olive oil mayonnaise

1 package (12 ounces) extra-firm tofu, drained, cut into eight ½" slices

4 whole wheat hamburger buns, toasted

4 small green lettuce leaves

1 large tomato, cut into 4 slices

1 small ripe avocado, pitted, peeled, and cut into slices

note: Soy sauce is one of the oldest condiments in the world. It's a mixture made from fermented soybeans and wheat with a brining process. The sauce is aged from 6 months (the type most commonly found in supermarkets) to many years (precious and pricey bottles). Also found in supermarkets are chemically made soy sauces. They're made with hydrolyzed soy protein and flavored and colored with corn syrup, caramel, water, and salt. Read the ingredient list before you grab your next bottle.

per serving: 434 calories, 14 g protein, 34 g carbohydrates, 28 g fat, 4 g saturated fat, 8 g fiber, 743 mg sodium

portobello "philly" sandwich

prep time: 15 minutes • **total time:** 40 minutes

1. Heat 2 tablespoons of the oil in a large skillet over medium-high heat. Cook the onion and bell peppers, stirring often, for 5 minutes, or until softened. Stir in the vinegar, garlic, salt, and black pepper and cook for 1 minute. Transfer to a medium bowl.

2. In the same skillet, heat the remaining oil. Cook the mushrooms for 8 minutes, turning once, or until the juices are released. Drain off any juices. Stir in the bell pepper mixture and the spinach, cover, and turn off the heat. Let sit for 4 minutes, or until the spinach wilts.

3. Preheat the broiler. Slice open and hollow out the hoagie rolls, reserving the center pieces for another use. Place the rolls open on a baking sheet. Evenly divide the mushroom mixture among the rolls. Top with the cheese slices. Broil the sandwiches 8" from the heat source for 2 minutes, or until the cheese melts.

makes 4 servings

¼ cup extra-virgin olive oil, divided

1 large sweet onion, thinly sliced

2 red and/or green bell peppers, thinly sliced

2 tablespoons white wine vinegar

3 cloves garlic, minced

¼ teaspoon sea salt

¼ teaspoon pepper

6 portobello mushrooms (4" to 5" diameter), stems removed, and halved

½ package (6 ounces) baby spinach, about 3 cups

4 hoagie or sub rolls (about 7" each)

4 slices (1 ounce each) provolone cheese, halved

healthy know-how

If you're thinking that you'll be missing the meat in our take on this classic, think again. The reduced moisture of portobello mushrooms enriches the taste and creates a meaty flavor.

per serving: 500 calories, 18 g protein, 52 g carbohydrates, 26 g fat, 8 g saturated fat, 7 g fiber, 805 mg sodium

smoky meatless sloppy joes

prep time: 15 minutes • **total time:** 25 minutes

2 cloves garlic

1 onion, cut into large chunks

1 green bell pepper, cut into large chunks

1 tablespoon extra-virgin olive oil

1 package (10 ounces) baby bella mushrooms, halved

⅓ cup sunflower seeds

1 tablespoon tomato paste

1 tablespoon chili powder

¾ cup canned tomato sauce

¼ cup canned chipotle pepper sauce (medium heat)

1 tablespoon honey

1 tablespoon Worcestershire sauce

4 whole grain hamburger buns

1. In a food processor, finely chop the garlic. Add the onion and bell pepper and process until chopped.

2. Heat the oil in a large skillet over medium heat. Cook the onion mixture for 5 minutes, or until almost softened. Meanwhile, add the mushrooms and sunflower seeds to the processor and, using short bursts, process just until chopped.

3. Add the mushroom mixture to the skillet and cook, stirring, for 5 minutes. Stir in the tomato paste and chili powder. Add the tomato and chipotle sauces, honey, and Worcestershire. Cook for 3 minutes, or until thickened slightly. Divide the buns and sloppy Joe mixture among 4 plates.

makes 4 servings

healthy know-how

Even though you may think they taste the same, not all peppers are digested the same way in everyone's bodies. If you have a hard time digesting green bell peppers, choose one of their sweeter varieties, such as a red, yellow, or orange bell pepper.

per serving: 413 calories, 14 g protein, 65 g carbohydrates, 13 g fat, 1 g saturated fat, 6 g fiber, 830 mg sodium

caramelized onion and fennel pizza

prep time: 10 minutes • **total time:** 50 minutes

1. Preheat the oven to 450°F. On a baking sheet or roasting pan, combine the onion, fennel, tomatoes, and garlic. Add the oil, rosemary, and red pepper flakes. Toss to coat well.

2. Roast for 25 minutes, stirring occasionally, or until the vegetables are tender and lightly browned.

3. In a medium bowl, mash the beans until coarsely mashed. Spread evenly over the pizza crust, leaving a ½" border. Scatter the vegetables over the top. Sprinkle with the cheese. Bake for 10 minutes, or until the topping is hot and the crust is crisp. Let stand for 5 minutes before cutting into 6 slices.

makes 6 servings

1 large red onion, cut into 8 wedges

1 small fennel bulb, thinly sliced

2 plum tomatoes, chopped

3 cloves garlic, thinly sliced

1 tablespoon extra-virgin olive oil

1 tablespoon chopped fresh rosemary or 1 teaspoon dried

¼ teaspoon red pepper flakes

1 cup cannellini beans, rinsed and drained

1 thin whole wheat pizza crust (11" diameter)

2 ounces reduced-fat goat cheese, crumbled

per serving: 261 calories, 10 g protein, 36 g carbohydrates, 7 g fat, 3 g saturated fat, 7 g fiber, 361 mg sodium

caribbean chicken and vegetable soup

prep time: 10 minutes • **total time:** 45 minutes

2 tablespoons extra-virgin olive oil, divided

¾ pound boneless, skinless chicken thighs, cut into ¾" pieces

1 large onion, chopped

¼ cup water

1 can (14.5 ounces) diced tomatoes, drained

1¼ cups coconut milk

1½ teaspoons jerk seasoning

1 large sweet potato, cut into ½" pieces

½ small cauliflower, cut into small florets (about 3 cups)

4 cups (4 ounces) coarsely chopped kale

¼ cup chopped fresh cilantro

Lime wedges, for serving

1. Heat 1 tablespoon of the oil in a Dutch oven over medium heat. Cook the chicken for 10 minutes, or until browned, turning once. Remove the chicken to a plate and set aside. Add the onion, water, and the remaining 1 tablespoon oil. Cook for 5 minutes, stirring occasionally, or until softened.

2. Stir in the tomatoes, coconut milk, and jerk seasoning until combined. Add the sweet potato and cauliflower, pressing down to submerge in the liquid. Cover and simmer for 10 minutes. Stir in the kale and chicken; cook for 10 minutes, or until the vegetables are tender. Sprinkle with the cilantro and serve with the lime wedges.

makes 4 servings

tip: Since jerk spice blends can vary in heat and flavor profiles, add the seasoning gradually and adjust the amount to your liking. If your seasoning doesn't contain salt, add ¼ teaspoon salt with the seasoning.

per serving: 393 calories, 22 g protein, 22 g carbohydrates, 26 g fat, 15 g saturated fat, 5 g fiber, 391 mg sodium

curried lentil soup

prep time: 15 minutes • total time: 50 minutes

1. Heat the oil in a large saucepot over medium heat. Cook the onion, stirring frequently, for 5 minutes, or until softened. Stir in the celery, carrot, curry, and turmeric and cook for 1 minute, or until fragrant. Add the broth and lentils. Increase the heat to medium-high and bring to a boil. Reduce the heat to low, cover, and cook for 10 minutes.

2. Stir in the cauliflower and salt, cover, and cook for 20 minutes, or until the cauliflower is softened and the lentils are cooked. Serve with the pita, if using.

makes 4 servings

1 tablespoon extra-virgin olive oil

1 small onion, diced

2 ribs celery, trimmed and sliced

1 large carrot, sliced

1 tablespoon mild curry powder

2 teaspoons ground turmeric

1 container (32 ounces) reduced-sodium vegetable broth

1 cup red lentils

2½ cups cauliflower florets

½ teaspoon sea salt

Toasted whole wheat pita bread (optional)

healthy know-how

Curry dishes have a lot of flavor, but if it's your first time using this spice, it may be a challenge to execute the proper taste. Eliminate the raw taste of curry powder by sautéing it in a little olive oil before adding it to a dish.

per 1½-cup serving: 262 calories, 15 g protein, 40 g carbohydrates, 5 g fat, 0.5 g saturated fat, 11 g fiber, 384 mg sodium

fiesta turkey soup

prep time: 10 minutes • **total time:** 50 minutes

1 tablespoon extra-virgin olive oil

1 onion, chopped

1 small jalapeño pepper, seeded and finely chopped (wear plastic gloves when handling)

1 medium zucchini, chopped

2 teaspoons ground cumin

½ teaspoon ancho chili powder

1 pound 99% fat-free ground turkey

1 package (32 ounces) low-sodium chicken broth

1 can (14.5 ounces) diced tomatoes

1 can (15 ounces) black beans, rinsed and drained

1 cup frozen corn kernels

½ cup chopped fresh cilantro

6 tablespoons shredded Cheddar cheese

½ avocado, chopped

1. In a large saucepan, heat the oil over medium-high heat. Cook the onion and jalapeño, stirring occasionally, for 5 minutes, or until lightly browned. Stir in the zucchini, cumin, and chili powder. Cook for 10 minutes, or until the zucchini is lightly browned. Add the turkey and cook, stirring to break up with a spoon, for 5 minutes, or until no longer pink.

2. Stir in the broth, tomatoes (with juice), beans, and corn. Bring to a boil over high heat. Reduce the heat to low and simmer for 20 minutes, or until the liquid has reduced by one-quarter. Remove from the heat.

3. Stir in the cilantro. Divide among 6 bowls. Sprinkle each serving with 1 tablespoon of the cheese. Serve with the avocado.

makes 6 servings

per serving: 248 calories, 25 g protein, 21 g carbohydrates, 8 g fat, 2 g saturated fat, 5 g fiber, 512 mg sodium

creamy broccoli soup
with parmesan crisps

prep time: 15 minutes • **total time:** 40 minutes

1. Place the wrap on a baking sheet and sprinkle with the cheese, spreading it out until near the edges.

2. In a small saucepan, heat the broth and milk until almost simmering. Meanwhile, heat the oil in a large saucepan over medium heat. Cook the onion and garlic for 5 minutes, or until translucent. Add the flour and cook, stirring, for 1 minute. Add the hot broth mixture and simmer for 5 minutes, stirring constantly with a whisk, or until the mixture thickens. Add the broccoli and cook for 5 minutes, or until tender. Remove from the heat and cool slightly.

3. Preheat the oven to 400°F. Transfer the mixture to a blender or food processor. Add the parsley, thyme, and pepper. Puree until smooth, in batches as necessary.

4. Return the soup to the saucepan and reheat just to boiling. Bake the wrap for 8 to 10 minutes, until the cheese is melted and the wrap is crisp. Immediately cut into 8 wedges. Serve the soup with the Parmesan crisps.

makes 4 servings

1 multigrain wrap (8" diameter)

⅓ cup grated Parmesan cheese

2 cups reduced-sodium chicken broth

1 cup 1% milk

2 teaspoons extra-virgin olive oil

1 cup chopped onion

2 cloves garlic, minced

2 tablespoons flour

6 cups chopped broccoli florets and peeled stems, steamed to tender-crisp

½ packed cup Italian parsley, chopped

1 tablespoon fresh thyme, chopped

½ teaspoon pepper

per serving: 185 calories, 12 g protein, 26 g carbohydrates, 6 g fat, 2 g saturated fat, 5 g fiber, 445 mg sodium

hearty minestrone soup

prep time: 20 minutes • total time: 40 minutes

2 tablespoons extra-virgin olive oil

1 small onion, diced

2 cloves garlic, minced

1 package (8 ounces) sliced cremini (or baby bella) mushrooms

1 tablespoon chopped fresh rosemary

2 ribs celery, thinly sliced

2 carrots, diced

1 cup green beans, trimmed and cut into 1" pieces

1 container (32 ounces) reduced-sodium vegetable broth

1 can (14.5 ounces) crushed tomatoes

½ cup ditalini or any small pasta

1½ cups small cauliflower florets

1 can (14 ounces) cannellini beans, rinsed and drained

1. Heat the oil in a large saucepot over medium heat. Cook the onion, stirring frequently, for 5 minutes, or until translucent. Stir in the garlic and cook for 30 seconds. Add the mushrooms and rosemary and cook, stirring occasionally, for 5 minutes, or until the vegetables soften. Add the celery, carrots, and green beans. Stir in the broth. Increase the heat to medium-high and bring to a boil.

2. Stir in the tomatoes, pasta, and cauliflower. Return the mixture to a boil and cook for 5 minutes. Add the cannellini beans and reduce the heat to low. Simmer for 10 minutes, or until the pasta is al dente.

makes 6 servings

per serving: 185 calories, 7 g protein, 28 g carbohydrates, 5 g fat, 1 g saturated fat, 6 g fiber, 336 mg sodium

butternut squash–ginger soup

prep time: 15 minutes • **total time:** 45 minutes

1. Heat the oil in a large saucepot over medium heat. Cook the onion and ginger, stirring frequently, for 5 minutes, or until the onion is translucent. Add the broth, squash, salt, and pepper. Increase the heat to medium-high and bring to a boil. Reduce the heat to medium-low and cook for 20 minutes, or until the squash is fork-tender. Let cool for 5 minutes (see Note).

2. Working in batches, puree the soup in a blender. Return the soup to the saucepot. Stir in the honey and heat over low heat to warm through. Serve topped with the apple and pumpkin seeds, if using.

makes 4 servings

note: Hot soup expands faster than a cooled liquid. To avoid a blender blunder, fill the base only halfway. Remove the center of the lid to allow steam to escape. Cover the lid with a folded kitchen towel and then puree the soup.

- 2 tablespoons extra-virgin olive oil
- 1 large sweet onion, diced
- 1 piece (2") fresh ginger, peeled and cut into 4 pieces
- 1 container (32 ounces) reduced-sodium vegetable broth
- 1 butternut squash (2½ pounds), peeled, seeded, and cubed
- ½ teaspoon sea salt
- ¼ teaspoon pepper
- 1 tablespoon honey
- 1 small apple, seeded and diced

  Pumpkin seeds, toasted (optional)

per serving: 209 calories, 2 g protein, 36 g carbohydrates, 7 g fat, 1 g saturated fat, 5 g fiber, 338 mg sodium

basic chicken broth

When making this broth, if you want some of the chicken meat for use in a soup, remove the breast and thigh meat after 1 hour. Return all the trimmings to the pot and continue simmering.

4	pounds chicken parts
4	quarts cold water
2	onions, quartered
2	celery ribs, sliced
2	small carrots, sliced
6 to 8	parsley sprigs
4	whole peppercorns
4	cloves
2	bay leaves
1	teaspoon dried thyme
1	tablespoon vinegar
½	teaspoon salt

1. Cut a few gashes in the chicken parts. Place in a large stockpot or Dutch oven over medium heat. Add the water and bring to a simmer. Reduce the heat to low and cook for 15 minutes, skimming any foam from the surface.

2. Add the onions, celery, carrots, parsley, peppercorns, cloves, bay leaves, thyme, vinegar, and salt. Simmer gently for 3 to 5 hours, adding more water, if necessary, to keep the chicken covered.

3. Scoop out the largest pieces of chicken with a slotted spoon and transfer them to a large colander set over a large bowl. Drain and discard the pieces (the chicken meat will be dried out and flavorless). Strain the broth and discard all solids. If desired, strain again through a finer sieve. Refrigerate the broth overnight. Skim off and discard the fat on the surface. For double-strength broth or a glaze, return the broth to a saucepan and simmer until reduced by half (for double-strength broth) or by three-quarters (for glaze).

makes about 2 quarts

apple–sweet potato soup

prep time: 10 minutes • **total time:** 8 hours 20 minutes

1. In a 4-quart or larger slow cooker, place the sweet potatoes, apples, onion, thyme, and broth and stir to combine.

2. Cover and cook on low for 8 hours, or on high for 4 hours, until the sweet potatoes are tender. Let cool slightly, about 10 minutes. In a blender or food processor, puree the soup until smooth.

makes 8 servings

5 sweet potatoes (2 pounds), peeled and cut into chunks

2 Granny Smith apples, cored and quartered

1 onion, finely chopped

1 teaspoon chopped fresh thyme or ⅓ teaspoon dried

5½ cups chicken or vegetable broth

per serving: 99 calories, 2 g protein, 23 g carbohydrates, 0 g fat, 0 g saturated fat, 4 g fiber, 385 mg sodium

beet, walnut, and pear salad

prep time: 20 minutes • total time: 20 minutes

1. In a large bowl, whisk together the oil, vinegar, mustard, coriander, salt, and lemon peel until blended. Add the pears and celery, tossing until coated well. Quickly toss in the beets just until combined.

2. Divide the salad greens among 4 plates. Spoon the salad mixture over the greens and top with the walnuts.

makes 4 servings

¼ cup flaxseed or extra-virgin olive oil

2 tablespoons apple cider vinegar or wine vinegar

1 teaspoon Dijon mustard

⅛ teaspoon ground coriander

½ teaspoon salt

½ teaspoon grated lemon peel

2 ripe pears, cut into thin wedges and halved

1 rib celery, diagonally sliced

4 cooked beets, cut into matchsticks

1 package (5 ounces) mixed salad greens

⅓ cup toasted walnuts, chopped

healthy know-how

The same old "beet-red" color can get boring if you're making a lot of dishes with beets in them. Change up the color of your basic salad by using beets in a different shade, such as pink, white, gold, or even two-tone striped beets. If you don't have time to cook the beets, peel them and shred them in the food processor.

per serving: 267 calories, 3 g protein, 22 g carbohydrates, 20 g fat, 2 g saturated fat, 5 g fiber, 378 mg sodium

warm sweet potato and lentil salad

prep time: 15 minutes • **total time:** 35 minutes

¾ cup French or small green lentils

2 cloves garlic, smashed

1 bay leaf

3 cups water

¾ pound sweet potatoes, peeled and cut into ½" pieces

4 scallions, sliced

¾ teaspoon salt, divided

3 tablespoons flaxseed or extra-virgin olive oil

3 tablespoons white balsamic vinegar or white wine vinegar

1 teaspoon chopped fresh rosemary

⅛ teaspoon pepper

1 package (5 ounces) baby kale greens

½ cup pomegranate seeds

1. In a large saucepan, combine the lentils, garlic, bay leaf, and water. Bring to a boil over high heat. Reduce the heat to low, cover, and simmer for 20 minutes. Stir in the sweet potatoes, scallions, and ¼ teaspoon of the salt. Return to a simmer and cook, covered, for 10 minutes, or until the lentils and potatoes are tender. Drain well.

2. Meanwhile, in a large bowl, whisk together the oil, vinegar, rosemary, pepper, and remaining ½ teaspoon salt. Add the drained lentil mixture and toss gently to coat. Toss in the baby kale or serve the warm salad over the greens. Sprinkle with the pomegranate seeds.

makes 4 servings

tip: If pomegranates are out of season, substitute ⅓ cup dried cranberries.

per serving: 317 calories, 10 g protein, 43 g carbohydrates, 11 g fat, 1 g saturated fat, 9 g fiber, 528 mg sodium

fennel and orange salad with tarragon vinaigrette

prep time: 20 minutes • total time: 20 minutes

1. In a medium bowl, whisk together the oil, vinegar, tarragon, mustard, honey, salt, and pepper until well combined.

2. Place the fennel in a large bowl. Using a sharp knife, slice off the top and bottom of the orange. Slice the skin away from the flesh, removing any white pith, and discard. Over the bowl with the fennel, cut between the membranes to segment the orange, allowing the juices and orange segments to drop into the bowl. Squeeze any excess juice out of the orange. Gently mix the fennel and orange pieces to combine.

3. Add the salad greens to the bowl and mix to combine. Top with the walnuts and feta cheese. Drizzle with the dressing just before serving.

makes 4 servings

- 3 tablespoons flaxseed or extra-virgin olive oil
- 2 tablespoons white wine vinegar
- 1 tablespoon chopped fresh tarragon
- 2 teaspoons Dijon mustard
- 1 teaspoon honey
- ¼ teaspoon sea salt
- ⅛ teaspoon pepper
- 1 small fennel bulb, trimmed and thinly sliced
- 2 navel oranges
- 4 cups mixed salad greens
- ¼ cup chopped walnuts, toasted
- ¼ cup crumbled feta cheese

healthy know-how

When choosing feta, try to buy the authentic varieties made from sheep's or goat's milk, rather than commercially produced feta made with cow's milk.

per serving: 237 calories, 5 g protein, 18 g carbohydrates, 18 g fat, 3 g saturated fat, 5 g fiber, 308 mg sodium

heirloom tomato, avocado, and shaved manchego salad

prep time: 15 minutes • total time: 15 minutes

3 tablespoons lemon juice

1 teaspoon raw honey

¼ teaspoon sea salt

¼ teaspoon pepper

¼ cup extra-virgin olive oil

¼ cup fresh basil, thinly sliced

5 assorted heirloom tomatoes (about 2 pounds)

1 ripe avocado, thinly sliced

1 piece (2 ounces) Manchego or Parmesan cheese

3 cups mixed salad greens

Fresh basil leaves (optional)

1. In a small bowl, whisk together the lemon juice, honey, salt, and pepper. Slowly drizzle in the oil while whisking until well combined. Stir in the sliced basil.

2. Cut each tomato into 4 slices. Stack the tomatoes and avocado slices alternately on serving plates. Using a vegetable peeler, shave slices of cheese on top of the stacks. Drizzle with the dressing. Serve the salad greens on the side. Garnish with the basil leaves, if using.

makes 4 servings

healthy know-how

Heirloom tomatoes are unique in appearance and packed with flavor. Popular varieties include purple, bicolor, and striped, just to name a few. These heirloom tomatoes add a beautiful appearance to a dish that classic tomatoes can't offer.

per serving: 363 calories, 7 g protein, 17 g carbohydrates, 28 g fat, 7 g saturated fat, 7 g fiber, 245 mg sodium

chopped vegetable salad
with sardines and toasted pita crisps

prep time: 20 minutes • **total time:** 20 minutes

1. Preheat the oven to 400°F. Place the pitas on a baking sheet and toast for 5 minutes, turning once, or until lightly browned and crisp. Break into 1" pieces when cool enough to handle.

2. Juice half of the lemon into a large bowl. Cut the remaining lemon half into wedges.

3. Whisk the oil, salt, and pepper into the lemon juice. Add the lettuce, tomatoes, cucumber, radishes, scallions, parsley, and mint. Add the pita pieces and toss to combine. Evenly divide among 4 plates and top evenly with the sardines. Serve with the lemon wedges.

makes 4 servings

2	whole wheat pitas (6" each)
1	lemon, halved
2	tablespoons extra-virgin olive oil
¼	teaspoon salt
¼	teaspoon pepper
2	cups chopped green leaf or romaine lettuce
2	plum tomatoes, chopped
¼	English cucumber, chopped
8	radishes, thinly sliced
6	scallions, chopped
¼	cup chopped fresh parsley
¼	cup chopped fresh mint
3	cans (3.75 ounces each) wild sardines packed in olive oil, drained

per serving: 288 calories, 20 g protein, 18 g carbohydrates, 16 g fat, 2 g saturated fat, 4 g fiber, 724 mg sodium

barley, artichoke, arugula, and almond salad

prep time: 15 minutes • total time: 40 minutes

¾ cup pearl barley

4 tablespoons extra-virgin olive oil, divided

1 small red onion, thinly sliced

1 package (12 ounces) frozen artichoke hearts, defrosted, halved

2 cloves garlic, minced

¾ teaspoon sea salt, divided

⅓ cup orange juice

1 teaspoon grated orange peel (optional)

¼ teaspoon pepper

2 cups baby arugula

⅓ cup dried apricots, thinly sliced

¼ cup sliced almonds, toasted

1. Bring 3 cups of water to boil in a medium saucepan over medium heat. Cook the barley for 30 minutes, or until tender. Drain, rinse under cold water, and drain well. Transfer to a large bowl.

2. Meanwhile, heat 2 tablespoons of the oil in a large skillet over medium-high heat. Cook the onion for 5 minutes, or until just softened. Add the artichokes, garlic, and ½ teaspoon of the salt. Cook, stirring frequently, for 10 minutes, or until lightly browned.

3. In a large bowl, whisk together the orange juice, orange peel (if using), pepper, and the remaining ¼ teaspoon salt. Slowly drizzle in the remaining 2 tablespoons oil while whisking until well combined.

4. Add the barley, artichoke mixture, arugula, and apricots. Divide among 4 serving plates and top with the almonds.

makes 4 servings

healthy know-how

Almonds can be purchased in different varieties—smoked, raw, salted, and with a variety of other tasty seasonings. If you want to intensify an almond's flavor on your own, though, toast it in the oven.

per serving: 379 calories, 8 g protein, 49 g carbohydrates, 18 g fat, 2 g saturated fat, 13 g fiber, 359 mg sodium

cooking time for grains

Most grains are incredibly easy to cook. For those listed below, measure the water into a saucepan and bring to a boil (unless otherwise indicated). Add ¼ teaspoon salt and/or 1 tablespoon butter or oil if you like. Then stir in the grain and return to a boil. Reduce the heat to medium-low, cover, and simmer until tender. If necessary, drain off any excess liquid.

grain	amount of grain (cups)	water (cups)	cooking directions	yield (cups)
Barley, pearl	¾	3	Simmer 45 minutes	3
Barley, quick-cooking	1¼	2	Simmer 10–12 minutes	3
Barley, whole (with hull)	¾	4	Soak overnight in the 4 cups water; do not drain; bring to a boil; reduce heat, cover, and simmer 55 minutes	3
Buckwheat, groats (kasha)	⅔	1½	Add to cold water; bring to a boil; cover and simmer 10–12 minutes	2
Bulgur	1	2	Add to cold water; bring to a boil; cover and simmer 12–15 minutes	3
Cornmeal	1	2¾	Combine cornmeal and 1 cup cold water; add to the 2¾ cups boiling water; cover and simmer 10 minutes	3½
Farina, quick-cooking	¾	3½	Simmer 2–3 minutes; stir constantly	3
Hominy grits, quick-cooking	¾	3	Simmer 5 minutes	3
Millet	¾	2	Simmer 15–20 minutes; let stand, covered, 5 minutes	3
Oats, rolled, quick-cooking	1½	3	Simmer 1 minute; let stand, covered, 3 minutes	3

grain	amount of grain (cups)	water (cups)	cooking directions	yield (cups)
Oats, rolled, regular	1⅔	3	Simmer 5–7 minutes; let stand, covered, 3 minutes	3
Oats, steel-cut	1	2½	Simmer 20–25 minutes	2½
Quinoa	¾	1½	Rinse thoroughly, simmer 12–15 minutes	2¾
Rice, brown	1	2¼	Simmer 35–45 minutes; let stand, covered, 5 minutes	3
Rice, white	1	2	Simmer 15 minutes; let stand, covered, 5 minutes	3
Rye berries	¾	2½	Soak overnight in the 2½ cups water; do not drain; bring to a boil, reduce heat, cover, and simmer 30 minutes	2
Wheat, cracked	⅔	1½	Add to cold water; bring to a boil, cover, and simmer 12–15 minutes; let stand, covered, 5 minutes	2
Wheat berries	¾	2½	Soak overnight in the 2½ cups water; do not drain; bring to a boil, reduce heat, cover, and simmer 30 minutes	2
Wild rice	1	2	Simmer 45–55 minutes	2⅔

couscous and chickpea salad

prep time: 10 minutes • **total time:** 50 minutes

1. In a medium saucepan over high heat, bring the water and 1 teaspoon of the oil to a boil. Stir in the couscous. Remove from the heat and cover. Let stand for 5 minutes, or until the liquid is absorbed. Fluff with a fork.

2. In a large bowl, whisk together the lemon juice and the remaining 2 tablespoons oil. Add the couscous, chickpeas, tomato, bell pepper, olives, and nuts. Toss gently to coat.

3. Cover and refrigerate for 30 minutes to blend the flavors. Top the salad with feta cheese.

makes 6 servings

- 1½ cups water
- 1 teaspoon plus 2 tablespoons extra-virgin olive oil, divided
- 1 cup whole wheat couscous
- 1½ tablespoons lemon juice
- 1 can (15 ounces) chickpeas, rinsed and drained
- 1 plum tomato, chopped
- 1 red or yellow bell pepper, chopped
- 2 tablespoons chopped pitted Kalamata olives
- 1½ tablespoons pine nuts
- ⅓ cup crumbled feta cheese

per serving: 268 calories, 9 g protein, 37 g carbohydrates, 10 g fat, 2 g saturated fat, 5 g fiber, 262 mg sodium

thanksgiving salad

prep time: 10 minutes • **total time:** 40 minutes

3 medium sweet potatoes, peeled, halved, and sliced into ¼" half-moons

2 tablespoons extra-virgin olive oil, divided

⅓ cup pearl barley

3 tablespoons apple cider vinegar

1 teaspoon Dijon mustard

2 teaspoons honey

2 teaspoons chopped fresh rosemary

½ teaspoon salt

2 cups shredded cooked turkey breast (about 12 ounces)

⅓ cup dried cranberries

½ small red onion, thinly sliced

1. Preheat the oven to 425°F. In a roasting pan, combine the sweet potatoes and 1 tablespoon of the oil and bake for 30 minutes, until fork-tender.

2. Meanwhile, bring 1 cup of water to a boil in a small saucepan over high heat. Add the barley, reduce the heat to medium-low, and simmer for 30 minutes, or until tender. Drain, rinse under cold water, and drain well.

3. In a large bowl, whisk together the vinegar, mustard, honey, rosemary, salt, and the remaining 1 tablespoon oil. Add the sweet potatoes, barley, turkey, cranberries, and onion. Toss gently to coat.

makes 4 servings

per serving: 355 calories, 29 g protein, 44 g carbohydrates, 7 g fat, 1 g saturated fat, 7 g fiber, 461 mg sodium

main dishes

marinated broiled flank steak with sweet-and-sour beet greens

prep time: 20 minutes • **total time:** 30 minutes + marinating time

1 pound flank steak, trimmed of all visible fat

3 cloves garlic, minced

1 teaspoon chopped fresh thyme

2 tablespoons + 1 teaspoon extra-virgin olive oil, divided

4 tablespoons balsamic vinegar, divided

⅛ teaspoon salt

⅛ teaspoon pepper

10 cups beet greens, washed, chopped, and left damp

1 tablespoon sugar

2 teaspoons grated lemon peel

2 cups cooked couscous

1. In a resealable plastic bag, combine the flank steak, garlic, thyme, 1 tablespoon of the oil, and 3 tablespoons of the vinegar. Turn the bag several times to coat the meat and chill for 1 to 24 hours, turning occasionally.

2. Preheat the broiler. Coat a broiler pan with 1 teaspoon of the oil.

3. Remove the steak from the plastic bag and wipe off the excess marinade. Set the steak on the pan and sprinkle with the salt and pepper. Broil 5" from the heat source for 10 minutes, turning once, or until a thermometer inserted in the center registers 145°F for medium-rare. Place on a cutting board and let stand for 10 minutes before thinly slicing across the grain.

4. Meanwhile, heat the remaining 1 tablespoon of the oil in a large skillet over medium-high heat. Cook the beet greens for 2 minutes, stirring often, or until starting to wilt. Add the remaining 1 tablespoon vinegar and the sugar. Cook for 2 minutes, stirring, or until wilted. Remove from the heat and stir in the lemon peel. Divide the steak, greens, and couscous among 4 plates.

makes 4 servings

per serving: 313 calories, 30 g protein, 30 g carbohydrates, 8 g fat, 3 g saturated fat, 4 g fiber, 316 mg sodium

mustard-glazed pork tenderloin with braised cabbage

prep time: 15 minutes • **total time:** 45 minutes

2 tablespoons Dijon mustard

1 tablespoon honey

½ teaspoon pepper, divided

1 pork tenderloin (about 1¼ pounds)

1 tablespoon coconut or extra-virgin olive oil

1 small sweet onion, chopped

4 cups sliced green cabbage

¾ cup reduced-sodium chicken broth

½ teaspoon sea salt

1 tablespoon apple cider vinegar

1 red apple, cored and thinly sliced

1. Preheat the oven to 350°F. In a small bowl, combine the mustard, honey, and ¼ teaspoon of the pepper.

2. Place the tenderloin in a roasting pan. Brush 1½ tablespoons of the mustard mixture over the top and sides of the tenderloin. Roast for 30 minutes, or until a thermometer inserted in the center reaches 165°F and the juices run clear. Let rest for 5 minutes. Cut into slices.

3. Meanwhile, heat the oil in a large skillet over medium-high heat. Cook the onion, stirring frequently, for 5 minutes, or until softened. Stir in the cabbage and cook for 1 minute, until lightly browned. Add the broth, salt, and the remaining ¼ teaspoon pepper. Cook, stirring frequently, for 6 minutes, or until the cabbage wilts. Stir the vinegar into the reserved mustard mixture and add to the skillet. Stir in the apple, cover, and reduce the heat to low. Simmer for 7 minutes, or until the apple softens.

makes 4 servings

per serving: 262 calories, 32 g protein, 19 g carbohydrates, 7 g fat, 1 g saturated fat, 3 g fiber, 570 mg sodium

the good things in cabbage

White, green, red, and purple: Cabbages come in many colors. While they are available in markets year-round, the best cabbages arrive at the end of the summer and stay until winter's cold puts an end to the harvest. To choose the best cabbage, look for the heaviest heads with bright, firm leaves. Or check out the stem end. If it is dry and shows signs of cracking, it may have been sitting around for a while. Dry stems could also indicate that the cabbage grew in dry weather and may have a sharp, unpleasant flavor.

Cabbage has several sulfur-containing compounds, which break down when cooked and release hydrogen sulfide. We know this better as the stench of a rotten egg. The best solution to reduce cooking odors is also the quickest: Cut the cabbage finely and cook it fast, so that the sulfur never gets a chance to emerge. Quick cooking not only reduces odors, it also preserves the maximum amount of nutrients. Some varieties have more nutrients than others. Here's which varieties have what:

variety	appearance	nutritional benefit
Green cabbage	Grows in tight, dense heads with darker-green outer leaves	Higher in vitamin C than other varieties
Red cabbage	Grows in dense heads with red or purple leaves	Higher concentration of vitamin C than other varieties
Savoy cabbage	Grows in less dense heads with frilly, ruffled leaves and yellow-green color	Higher in calcium than other varieties
Napa cabbage (Chinese cabbage)	Grows in dense, oblong heads, with light-green leaves and wide, white, crunchy stems	Good source of vitamin A, folic acid, and potassium

speedy arroz con pollo

prep time: 15 minutes • **total time:** 40 minutes

1. Heat 1 tablespoon of the oil in a large deep skillet or a Dutch oven over medium-high heat. Cook the chicken for 7 minutes, stirring occasionally, or until browned and no longer pink in the middle. Transfer to a plate. Heat the remaining 1 tablespoon oil in the skillet. Cook the onion and bell peppers, stirring occasionally, for 5 minutes, or until softened.

2. Stir in the garlic, tomatoes, paprika, turmeric, and salt until combined. Simmer, covered, for 5 minutes. Stir in the rice, peas, olives, and chicken and accumulated juices. Cover and simmer for 5 minutes, or until the vegetables are tender. Serve with your favorite hot sauce.

makes 4 servings

2 tablespoons extra-virgin olive oil, divided

1 pound boneless, skinless chicken thighs, cut into 1" chunks

1 large onion, coarsely chopped

2 bell peppers, coarsely chopped

2 cloves garlic, chopped

1 can (15 ounces) petite diced tomatoes

1 teaspoon smoked paprika

$\frac{1}{8}$ teaspoon ground turmeric

$\frac{1}{2}$ teaspoon salt

1 package (12 ounces) frozen brown rice

1 cup frozen peas

$\frac{1}{3}$ cup stuffed green olives, sliced

healthy know-how

If you haven't tried brown rice yet, you don't know what you're missing. The high-fiber bran coating of brown rice gives it a nutlike flavor and chewy texture, making it a better choice over white rice.

per serving: 447 calories, 29 g protein, 44 g carbohydrates, 15 g fat, 3 g saturated fat, 6 g fiber, 990 mg sodium

pumpkin seed chicken breasts with bulgur pilaf

prep time: 15 minutes • **total time:** 45 minutes

¾ cup bulgur

½ teaspoon salt, divided

¾ cup pumpkin seeds

½ teaspoon chili powder

½ teaspoon ground cumin

½ cup all-purpose flour

2 large eggs

4 boneless, skinless chicken breasts

1 tablespoon + 1 teaspoon extra-virgin olive oil, divided

3 medium carrots, sliced into rounds

1 medium onion, chopped

⅓ cup dried cranberries

4 scallions, white and some green parts, thinly sliced

¼ cup chopped flat-leaf parsley (optional)

1. Heat the oven to 400°F. Coat a baking sheet with 1 teaspoon of the oil.

2. Bring 1⅛ cups of water to a boil in a medium saucepan. Stir in the bulgur and ¼ teaspoon of the salt. Return to a boil, cover, and remove from the heat. Let stand for 30 minutes.

3. Meanwhile, in a food processor, pulse the pumpkin seeds, chili powder, cumin, and the remaining ¼ teaspoon salt until coarsely ground.

4. Place 3 shallow bowls on the counter. Add the flour to the first bowl. Beat the eggs in the second bowl. Add the pumpkin seed mixture to the third bowl. Dip the chicken breasts in the flour, shaking off the excess. Dip in the egg, then press into the pumpkin seed mixture so the mixture adheres. Place on the prepared baking sheet. Bake for 15 minutes, turning once, or until golden brown and a thermometer inserted in the thickest portion registers 165°F and the juices run clear.

5. Meanwhile, in a large skillet, heat the remaining 1 tablespoon oil over medium heat. Cook the carrots, onion, and cumin for 5 minutes, stirring occasionally, or until partially softened. Stir in the bulgur, cranberries, scallions, and parsley, if using. Evenly divide the chicken and bulgur among 4 plates.

makes 4 servings

per serving: 561 calories, 45 g protein, 52 g carbohydrates, 21 g fat, 4 g saturated fat, 9 g fiber, 471 mg sodium

turkey and white bean chili

prep time: 10 minutes • **total time:** 40 minutes

1. Heat 1 tablespoon of the oil in a large saucepan over medium heat. Cook the turkey, stirring frequently to break up clumps, until browned. Transfer to a bowl. In the same skillet, heat the remaining 1 tablespoon oil. Cook the onion, stirring frequently, for 5 minutes, or until softened. Stir in the garlic, oregano, and cumin and cook for 1 minute, or until fragrant.

2. Stir in the turkey, chiles, broth, water, beans, tortillas, and salt. Bring the mixture to a boil. Reduce the heat to low and simmer for 20 minutes. Stir in the cilantro and avocado, if using.

makes 4 servings

2 tablespoons extra-virgin olive oil, divided

1 pound ground turkey

1 medium onion, chopped

4 cloves garlic, minced

2 tablespoons chopped fresh oregano

1 tablespoon ground cumin

1 can (4 ounces) diced mild green chiles, drained

1 can (14.5 ounces) reduced-sodium chicken broth

¼ cup water

1 can (15.5 ounces) cannellini beans

3 small (6" each) corn tortillas, chopped

¼ teaspoon sea salt

Chopped cilantro (optional)

Diced avocado (optional)

per serving: 353 calories, 30 g protein, 22 g carbohydrates, 16 g fat, 3 g saturated fat, 5 g fiber, 651 mg sodium

oven-roasted cod with brussels sprouts

prep time: 15 minutes • **total time:** 30 minutes

1 **pound Brussels sprouts, halved**

6 **large shallots (8 ounces), quartered lengthwise**

2 **tablespoons extra-virgin olive oil**

½ **teaspoon salt**

1 **teaspoon grated orange peel**

1 **tablespoon orange juice concentrate**

1 **tablespoon honey**

1½ **teaspoons reduced-sodium soy sauce**

1 **teaspoon grated fresh ginger**

4 **pieces cod or halibut (about 6 ounces each)**

1. Preheat the oven to 425°F. Arrange the oven racks in the upper and lower thirds of the oven. Coat a 1½-quart baking dish with cooking spray.

2. Mound the Brussels sprouts and shallots in the center of a rimmed baking sheet. Drizzle with the oil and salt. Toss the vegetables until blended; spread in a single layer in the pan. Place on the upper rack and roast for 20 minutes, or until tender, stirring once. Toss in the pan with the orange peel.

3. Meanwhile, in a small dish, stir together the orange juice concentrate, honey, soy sauce, and ginger. Arrange the fish in the prepared baking dish and spread with the honey mixture. Place on the lower rack and roast for 10 minutes, or until the fish flakes easily. Serve with the Brussels sprouts.

makes 4 servings

healthy know-how

Overcooking Brussels sprouts can cause bitterness and destroy vitamin C, so be careful when roasting them.

per serving: 311 calories, 36 g protein, 26 g carbohydrates, 8 g fat, 1 g saturated fat, 4 g fiber, 478 mg sodium

turmeric-marinated swordfish

prep time: 25 minutes • total time: 25 minutes

1. *To make the fish:* In a medium shallow bowl, combine the oil, garlic, lime juice, turmeric, and salt. Place the swordfish in the marinade, turning to cover both sides. Refrigerate while making the coleslaw.

2. *To make the coleslaw:* In a large bowl, whisk together the vinegar, oil, lime juice, honey, cumin, salt, and pepper. Stir in the cabbage and carrot.

3. Preheat a grill to medium-high. Grill the swordfish for 8 minutes, turning once, or until the fish is just opaque. Serve with the coleslaw.

makes 4 servings

note: Be sure to use a fork (instead of your fingers) when turning the fish in the marinade. Why? The intense bright golden-yellow color of turmeric saturates the food that it's blended with and colors the skin.

fish

- ¼ cup extra-virgin olive oil
- 2 cloves garlic, minced
- 3 tablespoons lime juice
- 1 tablespoon turmeric
- ¼ teaspoon sea salt
- 1½ pounds swordfish, cut into 4 pieces

coleslaw

- ¼ cup seasoned rice wine vinegar
- 3 tablespoons extra-virgin olive oil
- 1 tablespoon lime juice
- 1 teaspoon raw honey
- 1 teaspoon ground cumin
- ¼ teaspoon sea salt
- ¼ teaspoon pepper
- 4 cups shredded green cabbage
- 1 large carrot, shredded

per serving: 386 calories, 35 g protein, 8 g carbohydrates, 23 g fat, 4 g saturated fat, 3 g fiber, 272 mg sodium

horseradish crumb-crusted salmon with roasted asparagus

prep time: 15 minutes • total time: 30 minutes

1   pound asparagus

2½ tablespoons extra-virgin olive oil, divided

⅜   teaspoon salt, divided

¼   teaspoon pepper, divided

2   tablespoons jarred horseradish, drained well

2   tablespoons chopped scallions

1   teaspoon grated lemon peel

½   cup panko whole wheat bread crumbs

4   skinless, boneless salmon fillets (about 6 ounces each)

    Lemon wedges

1. Preheat the oven to 450°F. Coat a 2-quart baking dish with cooking spray.

2. Mound the asparagus on a rimmed baking sheet. Drizzle with 1 tablespoon of the oil, ¼ teaspoon of the salt, and ⅛ teaspoon of the pepper. Toss together until evenly coated, spread in a single layer.

3. In a small bowl, stir together the horseradish, scallions, lemon peel, and the remaining 1½ tablespoons oil until combined. Stir in the panko until evenly coated. Place the salmon in the baking dish and sprinkle with the remaining ⅛ teaspoon each salt and pepper. Spoon the panko mixture evenly on top of the salmon fillets.

4. Roast the salmon for 12 to 15 minutes, or until golden brown on top and opaque. Roast the asparagus for 10 to 12 minutes, or until tender when pierced with a knife. Serve the fish and asparagus with the lemon wedges.

makes 4 servings

healthy know-how

If able to, always choose wild salmon over farm-raised. Wild salmon has deeper, more complex flavors.

per serving: 379 calories, 38 g protein, 13 g carbohydrates, 20 g fat, 3 g saturated fat, 4 g fiber, 339 mg sodium

garlic shrimp and kale stir-fry

prep time: 15 minutes • **total time:** 25 minutes

1 cup quick-cooking brown rice

3 teaspoons toasted sesame oil, divided

1 pound peeled and deveined medium shrimp

4 cloves garlic, sliced

3 scallions, chopped

2 medium carrots, thinly sliced

1 medium onion, chopped

6 cups chopped kale

½ cup low-sodium chicken broth

1 tablespoon hoisin sauce

1. Prepare the rice according to the package directions, omitting any salt or fat.

2. Meanwhile, heat 1 teaspoon of the oil in a large skillet over medium-high heat. Cook the shrimp for 3 minutes, turning once, or until opaque. Transfer to a plate.

3. Heat the remaining 2 teaspoons oil in the same skillet over medium heat. Cook the garlic, scallions, carrots, and onion for 2 minutes, or until just starting to soften. Add the kale and cook for 2 minutes. Add the broth and cook for 3 minutes, stirring occasionally, or until the kale has wilted. Stir in the reserved shrimp and the hoisin sauce. Cook for 1 minute, stirring, or until hot. Serve over the rice.

makes 4 servings

healthy know-how

Nutrient-packed kale is an extremely popular leafy green, but it can be difficult to pick out a fresh bunch. Make sure to choose bunches of kale with vibrant colors and avoid ones that have a large amount of limp leaves.

per serving: 318 calories, 30 g protein, 39 g carbohydrates, 7 g fat, 1 g saturated fat, 5 g fiber, 311 mg sodium

sizing up shrimp

Shrimp are usually sold by "count" or size. The count, such as 16/20, refers to the number of shrimp you'll get per pound according to their size. It can be a little confusing; here's how to make sense of it.

size	shrimp per pound
Small	40–50
Medium	31–40
Large	26–30
Extra large	21–25
Jumbo	16–20

roasted salmon with tomato-basil lentils

prep time: 15 minutes • **total time:** 50 minutes

1. In a medium saucepan, combine the lentils, water, garlic, bay leaf, salt, and pepper. Bring to a boil over high heat. Reduce the heat to low, cover, and simmer for 20 minutes, or until the lentils are tender. Drain the lentils and transfer to a serving bowl. Remove and discard the bay leaf. Add the tomato, scallions, basil, lemon juice, and 1 tablespoon of the oil. Stir to combine. Cover loosely and let stand while making the salmon.

2. Preheat the oven to 425°F. Coat a baking sheet with 1 teaspoon of the oil. Cut the salmon into 4 equal portions. On a cutting board, chop the garlic. Sprinkle it with the salt and crush with the flat side of a chef's knife to form a paste. Mix the garlic paste with the lemon juice and oil and rub on the salmon. Place the salmon on the prepared baking sheet. Roast for 8 minutes, or until the fish is opaque in the thickest part. Serve with the lentils.

makes 4 servings

¾ cup small green lentils, picked over and rinsed

3 cups water

1 clove garlic, minced

1 bay leaf

½ teaspoon salt

¼ teaspoon pepper

1 large tomato, chopped

2 scallions, thinly sliced

¼ cup slivered fresh basil

1 tablespoon fresh lemon juice

1 tablespoon + 1 teaspoon extra-virgin olive oil

1¼ pounds skinned salmon fillet

1 large clove garlic

¼ teaspoon salt

2 tablespoons fresh lemon juice

per serving: 453 calories, 38 g protein, 26 g carbohydrates, 22 g fat, 4 g saturated fat, 12 g fiber, 365 mg sodium

common sea vegetables

Here's a guide to the five most common types of seaweed. These are usually sold dried in packages in health food stores and Asian markets.

Kelp: Similar to Japanese kombu, kelp is sold in wide, dark-green strips. It is popular simmered in soups and stews as a salt substitute. To reduce the saltiness, rinse kelp briefly before using. Toasted kelp makes a crunchy addition to salads, stir-fries, and casserole toppings. Or add it to soups for rich mineral flavor and body, cooking it until softened. You can also add kelp to cooking beans to thicken them and promote easier digestion.

Dulse: When used raw, maroon-colored dulse cuts or tears easily and is chewy and slightly moist. For a crisper, more brittle texture, roast or fry it briefly. When cooked in liquid, dulse becomes very tender and will dissolve if cooked longer than 5 minutes. Use it in fish or clam chowders, fish cakes, and Caesar salads, or fry it in oil and use it in place of bacon in a BLT.

Nori: Also known as a laver, these green-black sheets are most often used to make sushi. Nori is also available in flakes, which dissolve immediately in liquid, thicken slightly, and lend a greenish color to soups. Try adding nori flakes to breading or savory piecrusts for a nutty flavor. Or use them to season salads or to add flavor and color to salad dressings. To make nori broth, simmer 1 part nori in 6 parts water.

Wakame: These long, dark-green strips are often added to soups and salads in Japan. Dried wakame strips, sold in the United Sates, should be soaked in warm water before using.

Hijiki: Dried into thin, green-black strips, hijiki is wonderful scatted over salads or stir-fries for savory crunch.

korean noodle bowl

prep time: 25 minutes • **total time:** 35 minutes

1. Grate the lime zest into a large bowl. Juice the lime (to make 3 tablespoons) and add to the bowl. Add the soy sauce, honey, oil, vinegar, and chili paste. Whisk together until blended.

2. Prepare the noodles according to the package directions, adding the shrimp during the last 2 minutes of cooking. Cook until the shrimp are opaque and the noodles are just tender. Drain and rinse under cold water. Drain well and add to the bowl with the lime mixture. Add the cucumber, scallions, carrots, and cabbage. Toss together until combined. Serve in shallow bowls, topped with the roasted seaweed strips.

makes 4 servings

tip: This tasty soup can be prepared up to 1 day in advance and served chilled. Prepare as directed, tossing the noodles and shrimp with the dressing and keeping the vegetables separate. Toss in the vegetables right before serving.

1 large lime

3 tablespoons reduced-sodium soy sauce

3 tablespoons honey

2 tablespoons toasted sesame oil

2 tablespoons apple cider vinegar or rice wine vinegar

2 to 3 teaspoons chili-garlic paste or gochujang

8 ounces dried soba noodles

1 pound large (26 to 30 count) peeled and deveined shrimp

½ cucumber, seeded and julienned

4 scallions, diagonally sliced

2 carrots, shredded (1 cup)

2 cups thinly sliced napa or green cabbage

3 tablespoons slivered toasted seaweed

healthy know-how

Soba noodles get their dark brownish-gray color from the buckwheat and wheat flours.

per serving: 343 calories, 26 g protein, 66 g carbohydrates, 9 g fat, 1 g saturated fat, 3 g fiber, 1,609 mg sodium

tuna noodle casserole

prep time: 25 minutes • **total time:** 50 minutes

1. Preheat the oven to 375°F. Coat a 2-quart baking dish with cooking spray.

2. Prepare the noodles according to the package directions, adding the broccoli during the last 4 minutes of cooking. Drain well and return to the pot. Meanwhile, heat the oil in a large skillet over medium-high heat. Cook the mushrooms for 5 minutes, or until the liquid has evaporated, stirring occasionally.

3. Reduce the heat to medium. Sprinkle on the flour and stir until combined. Whisk in the milk, stirring constantly, until the mixture comes to a simmer. Stir in the scallions, cheese, mustard, salt, and red pepper until combined. Remove from the heat and add the tuna, breaking up any large chunks with a spoon. Stir in the yogurt until combined. Add to the pot and stir together until blended. Spoon into the prepared baking dish. Cover tightly with foil.

4. Bake for 30 minutes, or until heated through.

makes 4 servings

8 ounces whole wheat egg noodles

1 package (10 ounces) frozen chopped broccoli

2 tablespoons extra-virgin olive oil

1 package (10 ounces) sliced mushrooms

¼ cup white wheat flour

1½ cups 2% milk

1 large bunch scallions, thinly sliced

½ cup grated Parmesan cheese

1 tablespoon Dijon mustard

¼ teaspoon salt

⅛ teaspoon ground red pepper

2 cans (5 ounces each) water-packed tuna, drained

1¼ cups 2% plain Greek yogurt

per serving: 600 calories, 49 g protein, 61 g carbohydrates, 19 g fat, 7 g saturated fat, 9 g fiber, 828 mg sodium

pasta with eggplant and chickpeas

prep time: 30 minutes • **total time:** 55 minutes

1 large eggplant (1½ pounds), sliced ¾" thick

3 tablespoons extra-virgin olive oil, divided

1 large onion, chopped

3 large cloves garlic, cut into thin slivers

1 can (28 ounces) crushed tomatoes

1½ teaspoons dried basil

¾ teaspoon fennel seeds, crushed

¼ teaspoon crushed red pepper flakes

1 can (15 ounces) chickpeas, rinsed and drained

¾ pound whole wheat penne

Slivered fresh basil (optional)

1. Preheat the oven to 475°F. Line a large baking sheet with foil or parchment paper. Place the eggplant on the baking sheet in a single layer, brushing both sides with 2 tablespoons of the oil. Bake for 20 minutes, or until tender and browned, turning once. When cool enough to handle, cut the eggplant into ¾" pieces.

2. Meanwhile, heat the remaining 1 tablespoon of oil in a large saucepan over medium heat. Cook the onion for 5 minutes, stirring occasionally, or until softened. Stir in the garlic and cook for 1 minute. Add the tomatoes, basil, fennel seeds, and red pepper flakes. Cook for 25 minutes, stirring occasionally, or until slightly thickened and flavored through. Stir the chickpeas and eggplant into the sauce and cook for 2 minutes, or until heated through.

3. Meanwhile, prepare the pasta according to the package directions, or until al dente. Stir into the skillet with the eggplant mixture. Divide among 6 bowls. Top with the basil, if using.

makes 6 servings

per serving: 415 calories, 13 g protein, 72 g carbohydrates, 10 g fat, 1 g saturated fat, 13 g fiber, 244 mg sodium

penne with garlicky greens and beans

prep time: 20 minutes • **total time:** 45 minutes

4 ounces whole wheat penne

1 tablespoon extra-virgin olive oil

1 onion, chopped

1 carrot, chopped

3 cloves garlic, minced

¼ teaspoon red pepper flakes

1 bunch (½ pound) beet greens, stems trimmed, cut into 1" pieces

1 bunch (1 pound) broccoli rabe, tough stem ends trimmed, cut into 1" pieces

½ cup water

1 can (15 ounces) cannellini beans, rinsed and drained

3 tablespoons grated Parmesan cheese

1. Prepare the pasta according to the package directions. Reserve ¼ cup of the pasta cooking water and drain.

2. Meanwhile, in a large deep skillet, heat the oil over medium heat. Cook the onion and carrot for 5 minutes, stirring, or until the onion softens. Stir in the garlic and red pepper flakes. Cook for 1 minute, stirring, or until fragrant. Add half of the beet greens, half of the broccoli rabe, and the water. Increase the heat to medium-high, cover, and cook for 2 minutes, or until the greens wilt. Stir in the remaining beet greens and broccoli rabe. Reduce the heat to medium, cover, and cook for 10 minutes, or until the vegetables are tender. Stir in the beans. Cover and cook for 2 minutes, or until the beans are hot.

3. Stir in the pasta and reserved pasta cooking water. Cook for 2 minutes, stirring, or until the pasta is hot. Remove the skillet from the heat and stir in the cheese.

makes 4 servings

per serving: 315 calories, 18 g protein, 50 g carbohydrates, 6 g fat, 1 g saturated fat, 13 g fiber, 422 mg sodium

asparagus, pea, and barley risotto

prep time: 10 minutes • **total time:** 50 minutes

1. Heat the broth in a large saucepan over medium-high heat, bringing it to a gentle simmer. Keep warm. Heat the oil in a large deep skillet over medium heat. Cook the barley, stirring, for 2 minutes, or until fragrant. Add the garlic and cook for 30 seconds, or until golden.

2. Stir in the wine and cook for 1 minute, or until almost evaporated. Add 1 cup of the broth and cook, stirring frequently, until most of the liquid has been absorbed. Stir in the white ends of the scallions. Continue cooking, adding ½ cup of the broth at a time, stirring until incorporated.

3. Add the asparagus and peas during the last addition of broth and cook until the barley and vegetables are al dente and the mixture has a slightly saucy consistency. (The total cooking time for barley should be about 35 minutes.) Stir in the remaining scallions and the thyme, salt, and pepper and cook for 1 minute, or until the scallions are wilted. Serve with the cheese, if using.

makes 4 servings

- 3½ cups reduced-sodium vegetable or chicken broth
- 2 tablespoons extra-virgin olive oil
- 1 cup pearl barley
- 2 cloves garlic, minced
- ½ cup dry white wine
- 1 large bunch scallions, sliced
- 1 pound asparagus, tips trimmed and stalks sliced ¼" thick
- 1 cup frozen peas, rinsed in a sieve under hot water
- 1 teaspoon chopped fresh thyme
- ¼ teaspoon salt
- ¼ teaspoon pepper
- ½ cup freshly grated Parmesan cheese (optional)

healthy know-how

Not sure where to cut when trimming your asparagus? Hold one end of the spear in each hand and bend the stalk. The spear will naturally break where the stalk becomes tough.

per serving: 383 calories, 14 g protein, 54 g carbohydrates, 11 g fat, 3 g saturated fat, 13 g fiber, 469 mg sodium

gnocchi with asparagus, spinach, and tomato

prep time: 15 minutes • **total time:** 35 minutes

1 package (16 ounces) whole wheat gnocchi

3 tablespoons extra-virgin olive oil

1 medium sweet onion, diced

3 cloves garlic, minced

¾ pound asparagus, trimmed and cut into 1" pieces

1 large tomato, chopped

½ package (5 ounces) baby spinach (about 3 cups)

½ teaspoon sea salt

¼ teaspoon pepper

½ cup crumbled ricotta salata (see Note)

¼ cup chopped fresh basil

1. Prepare the gnocchi according to the package directions. Drain well.

2. Meanwhile, heat the oil in a large skillet over medium-high heat. Cook the onion, stirring frequently, for 5 minutes, or until softened. Add the garlic and asparagus and cook for 5 minutes, stirring frequently, or until the asparagus is tender-crisp.

3. Stir the cooked gnocchi, tomato, spinach, salt, and pepper into the vegetable mixture. Cover and turn off the heat. Let stand for 5 minutes, or until the spinach wilts. Evenly divide among 4 plates. Top with the ricotta and basil.

makes 4 servings

note: Ricotta salata is a variation of the creamy cheese that has been salted, pressed, and aged over 90 days. It has a mild, salty, nutty flavor and is ideal for crumbling, shaving, or grating into dishes.

per serving: 392 calories, 11 g protein, 56 g carbohydrates, 14 g fat, 4 g saturated fat, 8 g fiber, 880 mg sodium

italian stuffed portobellos

prep time: 10 minutes • **total time:** 60 minutes

4 **large portobello mushrooms, stems removed**

2 **tablespoons extra-virgin olive oil**

1 **onion, chopped**

½ **cup red quinoa, well rinsed**

2 **cloves garlic, finely chopped**

¾ **teaspoon Italian seasoning**

¾ **cup water**

8 **sun-dried tomato halves, chopped**

¼ **teaspoon salt**

¼ **teaspoon red pepper flakes**

1 **can (14 ounces) artichoke hearts, coarsely chopped**

⅓ **cup walnuts, chopped**

½ **cup fresh basil, chopped**

¼ **cup grated Parmesan cheese (optional)**

1. Preheat the oven to 400°F. Line a rimmed baking sheet with foil. Arrange the mushrooms stalk side up on the baking sheet.

2. Heat the oil in a saucepan over medium heat. Cook the onion for 5 minutes, stirring occasionally. Stir in the quinoa, garlic, Italian seasoning, and water. Simmer on low, covered, for 15 minutes. Stir in the sun-dried tomatoes, salt, and red pepper flakes. Cook for 5 minutes, or until the quinoa is tender. Remove from the heat. Stir in the artichokes, walnuts, and basil.

3. Evenly divide the mixture onto the mushroom caps and cover loosely with foil. Bake for 30 minutes, or until heated through. Sprinkle with the cheese, if using.

makes 4 servings

tip: To easily fill the mushrooms, fill a 1-cup dry measuring cup three-quarters full with the mixture, then invert onto the mushroom cap.

per serving: 277 calories, 9 g protein, 31 g carbohydrates, 15 g fat, 2 g saturated fat, 6 g fiber, 343 mg sodium

baked macaroni and cheese

prep time: 15 minutes • **total time:** 60 minutes

8 ounces whole wheat elbow macaroni

3 slices multigrain bread

3 tablespoons unsalted butter, divided

1 onion, chopped

2 cups 1% milk

2 tablespoons whole wheat flour

½ teaspoon dry mustard

¼ teaspoon salt

1½ cups shredded reduced-fat mozzarella cheese

1 cup shredded reduced-fat sharp Cheddar cheese

¼ cup grated Romano cheese

1 can (14.5 ounces) salt-free diced tomatoes, drained

1. Preheat the oven to 350°F. Coat an 11" x 7" baking dish with cooking spray. Prepare the pasta according to the package directions. Drain and rinse under cold water to stop the cooking, then drain again. Return to the pot. Meanwhile, place the bread into the bowl of a food processor and pulse it into bread crumbs.

2. Melt 1 tablespoon of the butter in a medium saucepan over medium heat. Cook the onion for 5 minutes, or until softened. Meanwhile, in a measuring cup, whisk together the milk, flour, mustard, and salt. Pour into the saucepan and cook for 3 minutes, whisking, or until the mixture begins to thicken. Stir in the mozzarella, Cheddar, and Romano and cook for about 2 minutes, or until melted. Pour over the pasta, add the tomatoes, and toss to coat. Pour into the prepared baking dish. Melt the remaining 2 tablespoons butter in a medium nonstick skillet over medium heat. Add the bread crumbs and cook for 1 minute, stirring, until coated with the butter. Sprinkle over the macaroni and cheese.

3. Bake for 20 minutes, or until bubbly and the top is golden.

makes 8 servings

per serving: 289 calories, 17 g protein, 36 g carbohydrates, 10 g fat, 6 g saturated fat, 5 g fiber, 233 mg sodium

side dishes

quinoa tabbouleh

prep time: 25 minutes • **total time:** 25 minutes

1⅓ cups water

1 cup quinoa, well rinsed

½ teaspoon sea salt, divided

3 tablespoons extra-virgin olive oil

2 tablespoons lemon juice

2 cloves garlic, minced

1 teaspoon grated lemon peel (optional)

1 teaspoon raw honey

2 medium tomatoes, chopped

½ small English cucumber, quartered and sliced

¼ small red onion, diced

1 cup fresh parsley, chopped

¼ cup fresh mint, chopped

1. In a small saucepan, combine the water, quinoa, and ¼ teaspoon of the salt. Bring to a boil over medium-high heat. Reduce the heat to low, cover, and simmer for 15 minutes, or until the liquid is absorbed. Let rest for 5 minutes. Fluff with a fork.

2. Meanwhile, in a large bowl, whisk together the oil, lemon juice, garlic, lemon peel (if using), honey, and the remaining ¼ teaspoon salt. Stir in the tomatoes, cucumber, onion, parsley, mint, and quinoa. Toss to coat well.

makes 6 servings

per serving: 188 calories, 5 g protein, 23 g carbohydrates, 9 g fat, 1 g saturated fat, 3 g fiber, 143 mg sodium

quinoa with raisins, apricots, and pecans

prep time: 15 minutes • **total time:** 35 minutes

1. Cook the pecans in a small skillet over medium heat for 3 minutes, stirring often, or until lightly toasted. Transfer onto a plate and let cool.

2. In a medium saucepan, combine the quinoa, orange juice, and water. Bring to a boil over high heat. Reduce the heat to medium-low, cover, and simmer for 12 minutes, or until the liquid is absorbed.

3. Transfer the quinoa to a large bowl. Add the apricots, raisins, scallions, cilantro, and toasted pecans. Add the oil, lemon juice, and salt, tossing to coat well.

makes 4 servings

3 tablespoons pecans, chopped

$\frac{2}{3}$ cup quinoa, well rinsed

$\frac{2}{3}$ cup orange juice

$\frac{2}{3}$ cup water

$\frac{1}{3}$ cup chopped dried apricots

$\frac{1}{4}$ cup golden raisins

2 scallions, finely chopped

1 tablespoon chopped fresh cilantro

1 tablespoon extra-virgin olive oil

1 tablespoon lemon juice

$\frac{1}{2}$ teaspoon salt

per serving: 254 calories, 5 g protein, 41 g carbohydrates, 9 g fat, 1 g saturated fat, 4 g fiber, 302 mg sodium

cajun rice and beans

prep time: 15 minutes • **total time:** 40 minutes

2 tablespoons extra-virgin olive oil

1 onion, chopped

3 cloves garlic, minced

2 ribs celery, thinly sliced

1 yellow bell pepper, thinly sliced

½ teaspoon smoked paprika

½ teaspoon dried thyme

¼ teaspoon ground red pepper

¾ teaspoon salt

¾ pound plum tomatoes, cut into large chunks

2¾ cups water, divided

1 can (15 ounces) kidney beans, rinsed and drained

1 cup quick-cooking brown rice

1 tablespoon red wine vinegar

1. Heat the oil in a large saucepan over medium heat. Cook the onion for 5 minutes, stirring, or until softened. Stir in the garlic. Transfer ¼ cup of the onion mixture to a medium saucepan and set aside.

2. Add the celery and bell pepper to the large saucepan and cook for 5 minutes, stirring, or until the vegetables soften. Add the paprika, thyme, red pepper, and salt and cook for 1 minute, stirring, or until fragrant. Add the tomatoes and ½ cup of the water. Bring to a boil. Reduce the heat to low, cover, and simmer for 10 minutes, or until the vegetables are tender, adding more water if necessary.

3. Meanwhile, add the beans, rice, and the remaining 1¼ cups water to the reserved onion mixture in the medium saucepan. Bring to a boil. Stir, reduce the heat to low, cover, and cook for 5 minutes, or until the rice is tender and the water is absorbed. Let stand for 5 minutes.

4. Divide the rice mixture among 4 plates. Stir the vinegar into the vegetables and serve over the rice and beans.

makes 4 servings

per serving: 247 calories, 8 g protein, 37 g carbohydrates, 9 g fat, 1 g saturated fat, 7 g fiber, 487 mg sodium

a guide to cooking dried beans, peas, and lentils

The cooking times are for beans that have been presoaked (except lentils and split peas, which need no presoaking). Use the water amounts as general guidelines, but to be safe, make sure the beans are covered by 1 to 2 inches of water.

1 cup dried beans	water (cups)	approximate cooking time	cooking yield (cups)
Adzuki	4	45–50 minutes	2½
Anasazi	4	1½ hours	2½
Appaloosa	4	1½ hours	2½
Black (turtle)	4	45–60 minutes	2½
Canary	4	1½ hours	2½
Cannellini	4	1½ hours	2½
Chickpeas (garbanzos)	4	2 hours	3¼
Cranberry	4	1½ hours	2½
Fava	4	45–60 minutes	2½
Flageolets	4	45–60 minutes	2¾
Greek elephant	4	45 minutes	2½
Kidney	3	1½ hours	2½
Lentils, green or brown	4	30 minutes	2¾
Lentils, red	3	20 minutes	2½

1 cup dried beans	water (cups)	approximate cooking time	cooking yield (cups)
Lentils, small (beluga, pardina, french)	3	25 minutes	2½
Lima	4	45–60 minutes	2½
Lima, baby	4	45–50 minutes	2½
Mung	4	1½ hours	2½
Peas, black-eyed	4	1 hour	2½
Peas, pigeon	4	1 hour	2½
Peas, split (green or yellow)	3	35–40 minutes	2¼
Peas, whole	4	1 hour	2½
Pinto	3	1½ hours	2
Red	4	45–60 minutes	2½
Soybeans	5	3 hours	2¾
White (green northern, marrow, navy, pea)	4	45–60 minutes	2½–3

veggie-fried brown rice

prep time: 15 minutes • **total time:** 35 minutes

2 eggs

1 tablespoon water

2 tablespoons grapeseed oil, divided

2 portobello mushrooms, halved and sliced

2 cups broccoli florets

1 carrot, shredded

1 rib celery, sliced

3 cloves garlic, minced

1 tablespoon grated fresh ginger

½ cup vegetable broth

2 tablespoons reduced-sodium soy sauce

2 cups cold cooked brown rice (see Note)

4 scallions, thinly sliced

1. In a small bowl, whisk the eggs with the water. Coat a large skillet with cooking spray. Heat the skillet over medium-high heat and scramble the eggs. Transfer to a medium bowl and set aside.

2. Wipe the skillet clean and add 2 teaspoons of the oil. Heat over medium-high heat and cook the mushrooms for 5 minutes, or until all liquid evaporates. Transfer to the bowl with the eggs.

3. Add the remaining oil to the skillet and heat over medium-high heat. Cook the broccoli, carrot, celery, garlic, and ginger, stirring constantly, for 5 minutes. Stir in the broth and soy sauce and simmer for 3 minutes, or until the vegetables are tender-crisp. Stir in the brown rice, scallions, mushrooms, and scrambled eggs. Reduce the heat to low and cook for 5 minutes, or until heated through.

makes 4 servings

note: A great go-to product to have on hand is the packaged frozen, cooked brown rice that you can find in the freezer section of your market.

per serving: 248 calories, 9 g protein, 31 g carbohydrates, 10 g fat, 2 g saturated fat, 4 g fiber, 727 mg sodium

ten ways to spice up rice

There's no reason to settle for bland, boring rice. Two or three seasonings can turn it into something special. For each recipe below, combine the liquid and seasonings in a saucepan. Bring the mixture to a boil, then add 1 cup raw rice. Reduce the heat to low, cover, and simmer until the liquid is absorbed, about 12 minutes (for white rice) or 40 minutes (for brown rice). Remove the pan from the heat and let it rest, covered, for about 10 minutes. Fluff the rice with a fork before serving. Each recipe makes 4 servings.

recipe	liquid	seasonings
Coconut Rice	1½ cups water and ½ cup coconut milk	2 tablespoons chopped shredded coconut, 2 teaspoons honey, ½ teaspoons salt, and a pinch of allspice
Cranberry Rice	2 cups water	¼ cup chopped dried cranberries, ½ teaspoon salt, ⅛ teaspoon ground ginger, and a pinch of cinnamon
Curried Rice	2 cups chicken broth	1 teaspoon curry power and 3 tablespoons dried currants
Garlic-Chive Rice	2 cups broth	1 clove garlic, minced, and 1 tablespoon minced chives
Ginger-Soy Rice	2 cups water	2 teaspoons *each* soy sauce and grated fresh ginger and 2 whole cloves
Lemon Rice	2 cups water	½ teaspoons salt, 2 strips lemon zest, and a pinch of nutmeg
Pesto Rice	2 cups vegetable broth	2 tablespoons prepared pesto
Quick Rice Pilaf	2 cups broth	¼ cup finely chopped carrot, celery, and red onion; ¼ teaspoon dried thyme
Tex-Mex Rice	1¾ cups broth and ½ cup prepared salsa	½ cup cooked black beans and 2 tablespoon cilantro
Turmeric Rice	2 cups vegetable broth	¼ cup minced green onion and ¼ teaspoon turmeric

mushroom-barley stuffing

prep time: 15 minutes • total time: 1 hour 30 minutes

1 ounce dried porcini mushrooms

2 cups hot water

2 tablespoons extra-virgin olive oil

1 package (8 ounces) sliced button mushrooms

2 ribs celery, chopped

1 large red onion, chopped

2 cloves garlic, minced

½ teaspoon dried rosemary

½ teaspoon dried thyme

2 cups pearl barley

3 cups reduced-sodium chicken broth

¼ cup chia seeds

2 tablespoons grated Romano cheese

¼ teaspoon salt

¼ teaspoon pepper

1. Preheat the oven to 400°F. Coat a 3-quart baking dish with cooking spray.

2. In a small bowl, combine the porcini mushrooms and water and let stand for 20 minutes, or until the mushrooms are soft. Using a slotted spoon, remove the mushrooms. Chop and set aside. Strain the liquid into a small bowl through a fine-mesh sieve lined with cheesecloth or a coffee filter. Set aside.

3. In a medium saucepan, heat the oil over medium-high heat. Cook the mushrooms, celery, onion, garlic, rosemary, and thyme for 10 minutes, stirring, or until the mushroom liquid has evaporated.

4. Add the reserved porcini mushrooms and the barley. Cook, stirring, for 5 minutes. Add the reserved mushroom liquid and the broth and bring to a boil. Remove from the heat. Stir in the chia seeds, cheese, salt, and pepper.

5. Place in the prepared dish. Cover and bake for 40 minutes, or until the barley is tender.

makes 8 servings

per serving: 217 calories, 7 g protein, 37 g carbohydrates, 5 g fat, 1 g saturated fat, 9 g fiber, 239 mg sodium

vegetable bread stuffing

prep time: 10 minutes • **total time:** 65 minutes

1. Preheat the oven to 325°F. Brush a 3-quart baking dish with 1 tablespoon of the oil.

2. In a large skillet, heat the remaining 3 tablespoons of the oil. Cook the onion, celery, bell pepper, and garlic, for 6 minutes, until the onion is translucent.

3. Transfer to a large bowl and stir in the bread cubes. Add the flaxseed, eggs, thyme, sage, salt, and pepper, and toss. Stir in enough broth to moisten the mixture.

4. Press the mixture evenly into the prepared baking dish. Bake uncovered for 45 minutes or until lightly browned and heated through.

makes 8 servings

- 4 tablespoons extra-virgin olive oil
- 2 large red onions, chopped
- 2 ribs celery, chopped
- 1 yellow bell pepper, chopped
- 1 clove garlic, minced
- 4 cups multigrain bread cubes (about 8 slices)
- ½ cup ground golden flaxseed
- 2 large eggs, beaten
- 1 teaspoon thyme, crushed
- ½ teaspoon sage
- ½ teaspoon salt
- ¼ teaspoon pepper
- 2 cups chicken broth, store-bought or homemade

per serving: 198 calories, 7 g protein, 18 g carbohydrates, 11 g fat, 3 g saturated fat, 5 g fiber, 415 mg sodium

whole wheat orzo with peas, asparagus, and toasted pine nuts

prep time: 15 minutes • **total time:** 40 minutes

1. Prepare the pasta according to the package directions, adding the asparagus and peas halfway through the cooking time. Drain.

2. To the same pot, add the oil, garlic, and thyme and cook over medium heat for 3 minutes, or until the garlic just starts to turn golden. Add the pasta and vegetables, broth, salt, and pepper. Toss the pasta until well coated with the garlic mixture and the broth starts to get absorbed. Remove from the heat. Stir in the cheese and sprinkle with the pine nuts.

makes 4 servings

- 8 ounces whole wheat orzo (1⅓ cups)
- 1 pound asparagus, tough ends trimmed, sliced ½" thick (about 2½ cups)
- 1½ cups frozen peas
- 2 tablespoons extra-virgin olive oil
- 3 large cloves garlic, cut into thin slivers
- 2 tablespoons chopped fresh thyme
- ½ cup reduced-sodium, fat-free chicken broth
- ½ teaspoon salt
- ½ teaspoon pepper
- ¼ cup grated Parmesan cheese
- 2 tablespoons pine nuts, toasted

per serving: 379 calories, 17 g protein, 56 g carbohydrates, 12 g fat, 2 g saturated fat, 10 g fiber, 214 mg sodium

kale, onion, and raisin sauté

prep time: 10 minutes • **total time:** 30 minutes

⅓ cup golden raisins

½ cup boiling water

2 tablespoons extra-virgin olive oil

1 large red onion, halved and sliced

2 cloves garlic, cut into thin slivers

1 bunch kale (about 14 ounces), thinly sliced

1 tablespoon balsamic vinegar

¼ teaspoon salt

¼ teaspoon pepper

1. In a small bowl, combine the raisins and boiling water to cover. Let soak for 10 minutes, or until plumped.

2. In a heavy Dutch oven over medium heat, heat the oil. Cook the onion for 10 minutes, or until softened, stirring occasionally. Stir in the garlic and cook for 1 minute, or until fragrant. Add the kale in 2 or 3 batches, stirring until wilted.

3. Stir in the raisins and any soaking liquid. Cover and reduce the heat to low. Cook for 5 minutes, or until the kale is just tender. Stir in the vinegar, salt, and pepper.

makes 4 servings

healthy know-how

Raisins have a habit of clumping together when they sit in a container for a while. To unstick raisins that have clumped, place in a small bowl and microwave on medium power for 40 to 60 seconds, checking every 10 seconds.

per serving: 147 calories, 4 g protein, 20 g carbohydrates, 7 g fat, 1 g saturated fat, 2 g fiber, 173 mg sodium

italian-style green beans with tomatoes

prep time: 10 minutes • **total time:** 20 minutes

1 pound green beans, trimmed and cut into 2" pieces

2 tablespoons extra-virgin olive oil

½ cup canned kidney beans, rinsed and drained

1 cup canned diced tomatoes

¼ teaspoon Italian seasoning

¼ teaspoon salt

¼ teaspoon pepper

1. Fill a large skillet with ¾" water and bring to a boil. Cook the beans for 5 minutes, or until just tender. Drain and return the beans to the skillet over medium heat.

2. Add the oil, beans, tomatoes, Italian seasoning, salt, and pepper. Cook for 3 minutes, stirring occasionally, or until flavored through.

makes 4 servings

per serving: 134 calories, 4 g protein, 15 g carbohydrates, 7 g fat, 0 g saturated fat, 5 g fiber, 338 mg sodium

choosing the right oil

Vegetable oil (usually soybean oil) is the most common oil reached for by home cooks, but another oil may be a better choice, depending upon the dish you're making. Here's what to choose when, including approximate smoke points for the best frying oils. *Smoke point* refers to the temperature at which an oil will begin to smoke and impart unpleasant flavors to food.

oil	characteristics	best uses
Almond	Toasted almond flavor; breaks down with heat	Dressings, cold desserts
Avocado	Rich, buttery flavor; breaks down with heat	Dressings, sauces
Coconut, virgin	Aromatic coconut flavor	Roasting, sautéing, stir-frying, baking
Grapeseed	Mild flavor, high smoke point (445°F)	Dressings, sautéing, frying
Hazelnut	Aromatic hazelnut flavor; breaks down with heat	Dressings, sauces, baking
Olive	Mild to rich olive flavor; pale-yellow to deep-green color; fairly low smoke point (410°F)	Dressings, sautéing, light frying
Peanut	Neutral flavor; golden color; high smoke point (450°F)	Stir-frying, sautéing
Pumpkin	Roasted-pumpkin-seed flavor; green color; breaks down with heat	Dressings, sauces
Safflower	Mild flavor; light texture; high smoke point (450°F)	Sautéing, frying
Sesame (toasted)	Strong, nutty flavor; breaks down with heat	Dressings, sauces
Walnut	Rich walnut flavor; amber color; breaks down with heat	Dressings, sauces, baking

spiced chickpeas with spinach

prep time: 5 minutes • total time: 15 minutes

3 tablespoons extra-virgin olive oil

4 cloves garlic, thinly sliced

2 teaspoons cumin seeds

¼ teaspoon coarse salt

⅛ teaspoon pepper

1 cup soft whole-grain bread crumbs (2 slices)

2 cups cooked chickpeas

¾ cup water

1 tablespoon plus 2 teaspoons white wine vinegar

5 ounces baby spinach leaves

1. In a medium saucepan, heat the oil and garlic over medium heat. Cook, stirring, until the garlic is translucent and fragrant, about 30 seconds. Stir in the cumin, salt, and pepper.

2. Add the bread crumbs and cook until the crumbs are toasted, about 2 minutes.

3. Add the chickpeas, water, and vinegar and simmer for 3 minutes. Stir, breaking up the bread to help it dissolve into the sauce.

4. Add the spinach and simmer, stirring occasionally, until wilted, about 2 minutes. Serve hot.

makes 4 servings

per serving: 353 calories, 13 g protein, 46 g carbohydrates, 14 g fat, 2 g saturated fat, 9 g fiber, 381 mg sodium

garlic-roasted asparagus

prep time: 5 minutes • **total time:** 15 minutes

1. Preheat the oven to 425°F. On a baking sheet, combine the asparagus, garlic, oil, pepper, and salt. Toss well. Arrange the asparagus side by side in a single layer.

2. Roast the asparagus for 10 minutes, or until tender, tossing once.

makes 4 servings

1 **bunch asparagus,** trimmed

3 **cloves garlic, minced**

1 **tablespoon extra-virgin** olive oil

⅛ **teaspoon pepper**

⅛ **teaspoon salt**

per serving: 52 calories, 2 g protein, 4 g carbohydrates, 3 g fat, 0.5 g saturated fat, 2 g fiber, 73 mg sodium

a guide to grilling vegetables

A hot grill brings out the best in many vegetables, infusing them with a sweet, smoky flavor. Start with a medium-hot fire. Toss vegetables with oil (seasoned, if desired) before grilling. For even cooking, leave space between vegetables on the grill rack (or grill screen, if using small vegetables). If any vegetables cook too quickly, move them to the side of the fire (known as indirect heat) and bunch them together. Cook all vegetables until tender and lightly charred.

vegetable	preparation	type of heat
Artichoke	Trim, blanch, and cut in half	Direct
Asparagus	Snap off tough ends	Direct
Baby carrots	Wash but don't peel; blanch	Direct
Beets	Blanch and cut into wedges	Indirect
Bell pepper, sliced	Core, seed, and cut into strips	Direct
Eggplant, sliced	Cut into ½"-thick slices; slice Japanese eggplant lengthwise	Direct
Eggplant, whole	Pierce in several places with a fork	Indirect
Fennel	Trim tops and peel fibrous strings; cut into wedges	Direct
Garlic	Slice off top of head	Indirect
Leeks	Trim, rinse, and remove tough outer leaves; halve lengthwise; blanch large leeks	Direct
Onions	Slice; secure slices with toothpicks	Direct
Portobello mushrooms	Wipe clean and remove stems; grill caps gill side up	Indirect
Potatoes, new, russet, or sweet potato	Microwave for 6 minutes. Cool and cut in half, quarters, or slices	Direct
Scallions	Trim root ends	Direct
Zucchini	Trim and slice lengthwise	Direct

grilled zucchini and edamame succotash

prep time: 20 minutes • **total time:** 35 minutes

1. Prepare the grill for cooking at 400°F, or heat a grill pan. Place the zucchini, bell pepper, and onion on a baking sheet. Drizzle with 2 tablespoons of the olive oil and season with the salt and pepper.

2. Transfer the vegetables to the grill and cook for 10 minutes, turning several times, until tender. Cool. Chop the bell pepper, zucchini, and onion.

3. Meanwhile, boil the edamame in water. Let cool.

4. In a serving bowl, whisk the remaining tablespoon of oil with the vinegar. Add the chopped vegetables and edamame and toss to coat.

makes 8 servings

1 medium zucchini

1 red bell pepper, stemmed, seeded, and halved

½ yellow onion

3 tablespoons extra-virgin olive oil, divided

¼ teaspoon salt

¼ teaspoon pepper

1 cup frozen, shelled edamame

1 tablespoon white wine vinegar

per serving: 145 calories, 5 g protein, 17 g carbohydrates, 7 g fat, 1 g saturated fat, 3 g fiber, 62 mg sodium

watermelon, cucumber, and jicama salad

prep time: 15 minutes • **total time:** 15 minutes

2 tablespoons lime juice

3 tablespoons honey

⅛ teaspoon salt

Pinch of ground red pepper

3 cups stick-cut seedless watermelon

½ medium cucumber, cut into 2"-long sticks (1½ cups)

1 cup matchstick-cut jicama

3 tablespoons chopped fresh mint

In a large bowl, whisk together the lime juice, honey, salt, and red pepper until combined. Toss in the watermelon, cucumber, jicama, and mint.

makes 4 servings

healthy know-how

To remove the skin of the jicama, cut off both ends with a knife. Then scrape the skin with the side of a teaspoon, moving from end to end.

per serving: 103 calories, 1 g protein, 27 g carbohydrates, 0 g fat, 0 g saturated fat, 2 g fiber, 77 mg sodium

honey mustard broccoli-cauliflower salad

prep time: 15 minutes • **total time:** 30 minutes

1. Preheat the oven to 475°F. On a large rimmed baking sheet, mound the broccoli and cauliflower. Drizzle with 1 tablespoon of the oil, the salt, and the pepper. Toss together until coated, spread in an even layer in the pan. Roast for 30 minutes, or until browned and tender, stirring.

2. Meanwhile, in a large bowl, whisk together until blended the honey, mustard, vinegar, coriander, and the remaining 1 tablespoon oil. Add the roasted vegetables and toss until coated. Serve hot or at room temperature.

makes 4 servings

1   pound broccoli, cut into small florets, stalks thinly sliced

1   medium cauliflower, cut into small florets

2   tablespoons extra-virgin olive oil, divided

½   teaspoon salt

⅛   teaspoon pepper

1½ tablespoons honey

1   tablespoon Dijon mustard

2   tablespoons white wine vinegar

½   teaspoon ground coriander

healthy know-how

Cleaning cauliflower takes longer than you think. Soak it in salted cold water for at least 30 minutes to flush out extra dirt.

per serving: 183 calories, 8 g protein, 26 g carbohydrates, 8 g fat, 1 g saturated fat, 8 g fiber, 487 mg sodium

middle eastern rice salad

prep time: 10 minutes • **total time:** 25 minutes

1. Bring 4 cups of water to a boil in a large saucepan. Add the lentils and reduce the heat to low. Simmer for 15 minutes, or just until tender. Drain well and cool.

2. Meanwhile, in a large bowl, whisk together the lemon juice, oil, lemon peel, paprika, and salt. Add the rice, carrots, celery, tomatoes, onion, and cooled lentils. Toss to coat.

makes 4 servings

1 cup brown lentils

3 tablespoons fresh lemon juice

2 tablespoons extra-virgin olive oil

1 teaspoon grated lemon peel

½ teaspoon smoked paprika

¼ teaspoon salt

1½ cups cooked brown rice

2 carrots, shredded

2 ribs celery, chopped

2 tomatoes, seeded and chopped

1 small red onion, chopped

per serving: 309 calories, 15 g protein, 55 g carbohydrates, 4 g fat, 1 g saturated fat, 9 g fiber, 197 mg sodium

sautéed red cabbage and pears

prep time: 5 minutes • **total time:** 25 minutes

2 tablespoons extra-virgin olive oil

1 large onion, sliced

½ red cabbage, thinly sliced

½ tablespoon fresh thyme or ½ teaspoon dried

⅓ cup water

2 tablespoons apple cider vinegar

2 tablespoons honey

1½ teaspoons grated fresh ginger

¾ teaspoon salt

1 large pear, coarsely chopped

1. Heat the oil in a large skillet over medium heat. Cook the onion, stirring, for 5 minutes. Stir in the cabbage, thyme, and water. Cook for 10 minutes, stirring occasionally, or until wilted.

2. Stir in the vinegar, honey, ginger, and salt until combined. Scatter the pear on top. Cover and cook for 4 minutes, or until the cabbage is tender.

makes 4 servings

healthy know-how

A lot of dirt can make its way in between the leaves of your cabbage. To make it easier, clean your cabbage by slicing it first, then placing it under running water.

per serving: 177 calories, 2 g protein, 30 g carbohydrates, 7 g fat, 1 g saturated fat, 5 g fiber, 467 mg sodium

vegetable roasting times

Almost any vegetable can be roasted, even greens. Winter squash takes on a wonderful flavor because the high heat enhances the vegetable's natural sugar. To roast any of the following vegetables, prepare them as necessary and roast on a lightly oiled, rimmed baking sheet in the lower third of a 450°F oven for the specified time. Toss any cut-up vegetables with 1 tablespoon of extra-virgin olive oil. The amounts are calculated for 4 servings.

vegetable	amount	preparation	roasting time
Asparagus	1 pound	Trim	10–15 minutes
Beets	2 pounds	Leave whole; scrub well	60–90 minutes; when cool enough to handle, slip off skins
Bell peppers	3	Cut into thin strips	10 minutes; stir halfway through cooking
Butternut squash	1	Peel and cut into 1" chunks	20–25 minutes
Carrots	1 pound	Cut into ½" sticks	18–20 minutes
Eggplant	1 medium	Cut into ½"-thick slices; brush with 1 Tbsp oil	20 minutes; turn slice over halfway through cooking
Green beans	1 pound	Trim	10 minutes; stir halfway through cooking
Potatoes and sweet potatoes	2 pounds	Cut into ½" chunks	30–35 minutes; turn halfway through cooking
Red onions	2	Leave unpeeled; halve; place, cut side down, on pan; cover with foil	25–30 minutes
Tomatoes	2 pounds	Use whole plum tomatoes	20–25 minutes; turn halfway through cooking
Zucchini	2 pounds	Halve lengthwise and cut into 1½" chunks	20 minutes; stir in halfway through cooking

roasted root vegetables with edamame

prep time: 20 minutes • **total time:** 60 minutes

1. Preheat the oven to 400°F.

2. In a rimmed baking sheet or roasting pan, combine the carrot, turnip, potatoes, and garlic. Add the oil, rosemary, thyme, salt, and pepper. Toss to coat well.

3. Bake for 25 minutes, stirring occasionally. Stir in the edamame and bake for 15 minutes, or until the vegetables are tender and the potatoes are lightly browned.

makes 6 servings

1 carrot, diagonally sliced

½ turnip, cut into 1" pieces

12 ounces Yukon Gold potatoes, cut into 1" pieces

2 cloves garlic, sliced

2 tablespoons extra-virgin olive oil

1½ teaspoons chopped fresh rosemary

1 teaspoon chopped fresh thyme

½ teaspoon salt

½ teaspoon pepper

¾ cup frozen shelled edamame

per serving: 123 calories, 4 g protein, 17 g carbohydrates, 4 g fat, 0 g saturated fat, 2 g fiber, 358 mg sodium

fingerling potato salad with creamy mustard-anchovy dressing

prep time: 15 minutes • total time: 30 minutes

1½ pounds fingerling potatoes

½ cup 2% plain Greek yogurt

6 canned anchovy fillets, finely chopped

2 tablespoons lemon juice

2 tablespoons grainy mustard

1 tablespoon extra-virgin olive oil

2 teaspoons honey

5 cups arugula

1½ cups cherry tomatoes, halved

1. Cut the potatoes in half (or in thirds, if large) crosswise on the diagonal. Fill a large pot with about ½" of water, insert a steamer basket, cover, and bring to a boil over high heat. Reduce the heat to medium, add the potatoes, cover, and steam for 10 minutes, or until fork-tender.

2. In a large serving bowl, whisk together the yogurt, anchovies, lemon juice, mustard, oil, and honey. Add the arugula, tomatoes, and potatoes and toss to coat well.

makes 4 servings

per serving: 241 calories, 10 g protein, 42 g carbohydrates, 5 g fat, 1 g saturated fat, 6 g fiber, 349 mg sodium

vegetable cooking times

vegetable	amount	microwave, high (minutes)	steamer (minutes)	pressure cooker (minutes)
Artichokes	4 medium	20–25	30–35	9–11
Asparagus	1 pound, trimmed	5–6	6–7	1–2
Beets	1 pound	12–15	30–35	20–22
Broccoli	1 pound, cut into florets	8–12	5–7	2–3
Brussels sprouts	1 pound	7–11	11–12	4–5
Cabbage	1 medium, cut into wedges	9–13	12–15	3–4
Carrots	1 pound, sliced	8–10	7–10	4–5
Cauliflower	1 pound, cut into florets	4–7	8–10	2–3
Corn on the cob	4 ears	10–14	10–12	3–4
Eggplant	1 medium, cubed	7–10	5–7	3–4
Green beans	1 pound	10–12	7–9	7–9
Kale	1 pound, 2" pieces	8–10	5–6	3–4
Leeks	1 pound, ½" slices	4–6	8–10	2–3

vegetable	amount	microwave, high (minutes)	steamer (minutes)	pressure cooker (minutes)
Mushrooms	1 pound, sliced	6–8	3–4	1–2
Onions, small whole	1 pound	6–8	15–20	4–5
Peas, green	1 pound, shelled	5–7	8–10	Not recommended
Peas, snap	1 pound	6–10	8–10	Not recommended
Potatoes, small whole	1 pound, pricked with fork	9–11	25–30	6–7
Spinach	1 pound	5–7	3–4	2–3
Squash, spaghetti	3 pounds, halved and seeded	7–9	25–30	6–7
Squash, summer	1 pound, sliced	4–6	8–10	2–3
Squash, winter	1 medium, halved and seeded	8–10	25–30	6–7
Sweet potatoes	2 pounds, pricked with fork	1–3	30–35	8–10
Turnips	1 pound, peeled and cut	7–9	10–12	3–4
Zucchini	1 pound, sliced	4–6	8–10	2–3

desserts and snacks

cantaloupe with honey-spiced yogurt

prep time: 15 minutes • **total time:** 15 minutes

1 small cantaloupe halved, seeded, peeled, and sliced

1 container (6 ounces) 2% plain Greek yogurt

1 tablespoon honey, plus more for drizzling

¼ teaspoon vanilla extract

⅛ teaspoon ground allspice

2 cups fresh raspberries

2 teaspoons finely chopped crystallized ginger

1. Evenly divide the cantaloupe among 4 dessert dishes.

2. In a small bowl, stir together the yogurt, honey, vanilla, and allspice until blended. Spoon over the cantaloupe and top with the raspberries and crystallized ginger.

makes 4 servings

per serving: 127 calories, 6 g protein, 25 g carbohydrates, 1 g fat, 1 g saturated fat, 5 g fiber, 37 mg sodium

pear crisp

prep time: 20 minutes • **total time:** 1 hour 15 minutes

8 ripe Bartlett pears (about 4 pounds)

½ cup dried cranberries

3 tablespoons raw honey

1 tablespoon grated fresh ginger

1 teaspoon grated lemon peel

½ cup all-purpose flour

1 cup old-fashioned rolled oats

¾ cup whole wheat flour

½ cup lightly packed brown sugar

1 teaspoon ground cinnamon

½ teaspoon sea salt

½ cup almond butter

2 tablespoons unsalted butter

1 tablespoon water

1. Preheat the oven to 350°F. Peel, core, and cut the pears into chunks. In a large bowl, combine the pears, cranberries, honey, ginger, and lemon peel. Sprinkle in the all-purpose flour and gently toss to combine. Pour into a pie plate or a 3-quart baking dish.

2. In a medium bowl, combine the oats, wheat flour, sugar, cinnamon, and salt. In a microwaveable bowl, combine the almond butter, butter, and water. Microwave on high power for 30 seconds. Stir until well blended and melted. Stir into the oat mixture until large crumbs form.

3. Sprinkle the topping evenly over the pears. Place the baking dish on a sheet pan and bake for 55 minutes, or until the topping is brown and the fruit is bubbly. Serve warm.

makes 8 servings

per serving: 454 calories, 8 g protein, 80 g carbohydrates, 13 g fat, 3 g saturated fat, 12 g fiber, 140 mg sodium

strawberry rhubarb cups

prep time: 15 minutes • **total time:** 25 minutes

1. Slice enough strawberries to make ½ cup. Quarter the remaining strawberries and divide between 4 dessert dishes.

2. In a medium saucepan, combine the rhubarb, honey, orange juice, ginger, and the ½ cup sliced strawberries. Bring to a boil. Reduce the heat to medium-low and cook for 5 minutes, or until the rhubarb is tender. Using a potato masher, mash to a saucelike consistency. Spoon the rhubarb mixture over the remaining berries to serve. (This can be made up to 1 day in advance, with the sauce and berries being chilled separately.)

makes 4 servings

1 **pound fresh strawberries**

1 **cup fresh or frozen rhubarb, cut into ½" pieces**

¼ **cup plus 2 tablespoons honey**

2 **tablespoons orange juice**

1 **teaspoon grated fresh ginger**

healthy know-how

Rhubarb is extremely tart and requires a lot of sugar. To reduce the amount of sugar, buy rhubarb that has a redder stalk.

per serving: 174 calories, 1 g protein, 46 g carbohydrates, 0 g fat, 0 g saturated fat, 3 g fiber, 4 mg sodium

watermelon ice pops

prep time: 10 minutes • **total time:** 6 hours

2 cups cubed seedless
   watermelon

2 teaspoons fresh lime juice

1 to 2 tablespoons honey

1. In a blender, blend the watermelon, lime juice, and 1 tablespoon honey. Taste and add additional honey if the melon is not quite sweet enough. (You will want it a little sweeter than normal.) Strain through a sieve to remove any small seeds.

2. Pour into 4 popsicle molds (3 ounces each) and freeze for at least 6 hours, or until solid. To make the pops in paper cups, insert popsicle sticks in the cups when the mixture is partially frozen.

makes 4 servings

per serving: 39 calories, 0 g protein, 10 g carbohydrates, 0 g fat, 0 g saturated fat, 0 g fiber, 1 mg sodium

chocolate almond cake

prep time: 20 minutes • **total time:** 50 minutes + cooling time

1. Preheat the oven to 350°F. Coat a 9" springform pan with cooking spray. Dust with 1 tablespoon of the cocoa. In a food processor, combine the blanched almonds and 2 tablespoons of the sugar. Pulse until finely ground.

2. Place the chocolate in a large microwaveable bowl. Microwave on high power for 1 minute. Stir until smooth; if necessary, microwave for a few more seconds to melt completely. Stir in the ground almond mixture, sour cream, egg yolks, butter, vanilla, ½ cup of the remaining sugar, and the remaining 2 tablespoons cocoa.

3. Place the egg whites and salt in a large bowl. Using an electric mixer on high speed, beat until soft peaks form. Gradually beat in the remaining ¼ cup sugar until stiff, glossy peaks form. Gently stir one-quarter of the egg whites into the chocolate mixture to lighten it. Fold in the remaining whites until no white streaks remain. Pour into the prepared pan and smooth the top.

4. Bake for 30 minutes, or until a wooden pick inserted in the center comes out with just a few moist crumbs. Cool on a rack. The cake will fall as it cools, leaving a raised edge. Gently press down the edge as it cools. Remove the pan sides and place on a serving plate.

makes 12 servings

- **3 tablespoons unsweetened cocoa powder, divided**
- **½ cup blanched almonds**
- **2 tablespoons plus ¾ cup sugar, divided**
- **3 ounces bittersweet chocolate, chopped**
- **½ cup reduced-fat sour cream**
- **2 large egg yolks, at room temperature**
- **1 tablespoon butter**
- **1 teaspoon vanilla extract**
- **5 large egg whites, at room temperature**
- **¼ teaspoon salt**

per serving: 174 calories, 4 g protein, 21 g carbohydrates, 10 g fat, 3g saturated fat, 2 g fiber, 84 mg sodium

creamy frozen coffee frappé

prep time: 5 minutes • **total time:** 5 minutes

2 teaspoons instant espresso or coffee powder

2½ tablespoons honey

½ cup low-fat evaporated milk, divided

1 cup ice cubes

⅛ teaspoon ground cinnamon

Combine the espresso powder, honey, and 1 tablespoon of the milk in a microwaveable glass measuring cup. Microwave on high power for 15 seconds, or until hot. Stir together until blended. Add milk to the measuring cup to equal ½ cup. Place in a blender with the ice and cinnamon. Blend for 1 minute, or until thick and smooth.

Mocha Variation: Add 4 teaspoons unsweetened cocoa powder to the blender with the ice and cinnamon.

makes 1 serving

per serving: 283 calories, 10 g protein, 59 g carbohydrates, 2 g fat, 2 g saturated fat, 0 g fiber, 152 mg sodium

chocolate fondue

prep time: 10 minutes • **total time:** 20 minutes

1. In a small microwaveable bowl or measuring cup, stir together the honey, milk, cocoa powder, and instant coffee. Microwave on high power, stirring once, for 1 minute, or until the mixture comes to a simmer.

2. Stir in the chopped chocolate until melted. Let stand for 10 minutes to thicken slightly. Serve with the fruit for dipping.

makes 4 servings

¼ cup honey

¼ cup evaporated milk

½ cup unsweetened Dutch-process cocoa powder

½ teaspoon instant coffee

2 ounces bittersweet or dark chocolate, chopped

Assorted fruit for dipping, such as apples, strawberries, pineapple, and/or cherries

per scant ¼-cup serving: 196 calories, 5 g protein, 32 g carbohydrates, 8 g fat, 4 g saturated fat, 4 g fiber, 18 mg sodium

brown rice pudding with papaya

prep time: 20 minutes • **total time:** 55 minutes + cooling time

2½ cups milk, such as soy, hemp, almond, rice, or dairy

⅓ cup honey

2 tablespoons packed light brown sugar

2 tablespoons chia seeds

1 egg

1 teaspoon vanilla extract

1 teaspoon grated lemon peel

¼ teaspoon salt

1 package (12 ounces) frozen brown rice

⅓ cup dried cherries or golden raisins

¾ cup chopped papaya

1. Preheat the oven to 375°F.

2. In a large microwaveable bowl, whisk together the milk, honey, sugar, chia seeds, egg, vanilla, lemon peel, and salt until blended. Stir in the rice and cherries or raisins until combined. Microwave on high power for 6 to 7 minutes, stirring every 2 minutes, until the mixture just barely begins to simmer. Spoon into the prepared a 1½-quart baking dish.

3. Bake for 35 minutes, or until the liquid is almost absorbed and the rice is very tender. Cool for at least 10 minutes. (Can be served warm or cold.) Spoon into dessert dishes and serve with the chopped papaya.

makes 6 servings (about 4 cups)

healthy know-how

Chia seeds can be stored for longer periods of time, since they have a very low fat content. These powerful seeds can be eaten plain or put on top of yogurt, cereal, or salads.

per serving: 270 calories, 8 g protein, 52 g carbohydrates, 5 g fat, 1 g saturated fat, 6 g fiber, 125 mg sodium

double dark chocolate pudding

prep time: 25 minutes • total time: 30 minutes + chilling time

¾ cup turbinado or raw sugar

½ cup unsweetened Dutch-process cocoa powder

¼ cup cornstarch

¼ teaspoon sea salt

2½ cups 2% milk

4 egg yolks

4 ounces bittersweet chocolate, chopped

2 tablespoons unsalted butter

2 teaspoons vanilla extract

⅓ cup heavy cream

2 teaspoons confectioners' sugar

¼ cup 0% plain Greek yogurt

1. In a medium saucepan, whisk together the sugar, cocoa, cornstarch, and salt. Whisk in the milk and egg yolks.

2. Heat the mixture over medium heat, whisking constantly, for 7 minutes, or until bubbles form. Reduce the heat to low and whisk for 1 minute, or until thickened.

3. Remove from the heat and stir in the chocolate, butter, and vanilla until smooth. Divide among 4 serving bowls. Cover the surface of the puddings with plastic wrap and refrigerate for 3 hours or up to 2 days.

4. In a medium bowl, using a hand mixer, whip together the heavy cream and confectioners' sugar for 1 minute, or until stiff peaks form. Gently fold the yogurt into the cream mixture and dollop among the pudding bowls.

makes 4 servings

per serving: 637 calories, 13 g protein, 74 g carbohydrates, 36 g fat, 19 g saturated fat, 4 g fiber, 201 mg sodium

honey-walnut biscotti

prep time: 20 minutes • total time: 1 hour 15 minutes

1. Preheat the oven to 350°F. Line a large baking sheet with parchment paper or foil.

2. In a medium bowl, whisk together the flours, baking powder, baking soda, and salt. In a large bowl, beat together the honey, sugar, oil, eggs, orange peel, anise seeds, and vanilla until blended. Stir in the walnuts until combined. Stir in the flour mixture in 2 additions, mixing until combined.

3. On the prepared baking sheet, spoon the dough into two 12"-long strips, spacing each 3" apart. Using floured hands, shape each evenly into 2½"-wide logs.

4. Bake for 20 minutes, or until golden. Slide the logs with the paper onto a rack. Let cool for 10 minutes. Reduce the oven heat to 300°F. Using a serrated knife, slice the logs crosswise into ½" slices. Arrange on the baking sheet, cut side down, and bake for 15 minutes, turning once, or until golden and crisped. Transfer to a rack to cool completely. Store in an airtight container for up to 1 week, or freeze for up to 3 months.

makes 50 cookies

- 2¼ cups white wheat flour
- ¾ cup buckwheat flour
- 1 teaspoon baking powder
- ¼ teaspoon baking soda
- ¼ teaspoon salt
- ½ cup honey
- ¼ cup packed light brown sugar
- ½ cup extra-virgin olive oil
- 2 large eggs
- 2 tablespoons grated orange peel
- 2 teaspoons crushed anise seeds (optional)
- 1 teaspoon vanilla extract
- 1 cup toasted walnuts, coarsely chopped

healthy know-how

Walnuts, when stored properly, can last a long time. Store shelled walnuts in the fridge for 6 months or freeze them for up to a year.

per serving: 80 calories, 2 g protein, 10 g carbohydrates, 4 g fat, 1 g saturated fat, 1 g fiber, 31 mg sodium

lemon–poppy seed loaf

prep time: 15 minutes • total time: 60 minutes

1. Preheat the oven to 350°F. Coat a 9" loaf pan with cooking spray. In a medium bowl, whisk together the pastry flour, all-purpose flour, poppy seeds, baking powder, baking soda, and salt.

2. In a measuring cup, combine the buttermilk, oil, lemon juice, lemon peel, and vanilla. In a large bowl, with an electric mixer on high speed, beat the eggs, egg yolk, and sugar for 3 minutes, or until thickened and pale yellow. Fold the dry ingredients into the egg mixture, alternating with the buttermilk mixture in 2 additions. Spread the batter into the prepared pan.

3. Bake for 45 minutes, or until a toothpick inserted in the center comes out clean. Let cool in the pan for 5 minutes and then turn out onto a rack. Cool completely.

makes 10 servings

1¼ cups whole wheat pastry flour

¾ cup all-purpose flour, plus some for dusting loaf pan

2 tablespoons poppy seeds

1 teaspoon baking powder

½ teaspoon baking soda

½ teaspoon sea salt

½ cup low-fat buttermilk

3 tablespoons extra-virgin olive oil

3 tablespoons lemon juice

1 tablespoon grated lemon peel

1 teaspoon vanilla extract

2 eggs, at room temperature

1 egg yolk, at room temperature

¾ cup turbinado or raw granulated sugar

per serving: 203 calories, 5 g protein, 32 g carbohydrates, 7 g fat, 1 g saturated fat, 2 g fiber, 225 mg sodium

caramelized chili-spiked pineapple sticks

prep time: 10 minutes • **total time:** 15 minutes

1 peeled and cored pineapple, cut lengthwise into 16 strips

¼ cup honey

2 teaspoons grated lime peel

½ teaspoon chili powder

⅛ teaspoon ground allspice

1 Lime wedge for serving

1. Preheat the broiler. Arrange the pineapple on a foil-lined broiler pan or heavy rimmed baking sheet. In a small dish, stir together the honey, lime peel, chili powder, and allspice. Spoon or brush the mixture evenly over the pineapple.

2. Broil 4" from the heat source for 4 minutes, or until the pineapple is just caramelized around the edges and tender. Serve with the lime wedges.

makes 4 servings

healthy know-how

Unlike many other fruits, pineapple must get picked when it's ripe. The starch found in pineapples will not turn into sugar once the fruit is picked from the plant.

per serving: 90 calories, 1 g protein, 24 g carbohydrates, 0 g fat, 0 g saturated fat, 2 g fiber, 2 mg sodium

papaya-tomato bruschetta

prep time: 10 minutes • **total time:** 20 minutes

1 whole wheat baguette, cut into 24 slices (½" thick)

2 tablespoons extra-virgin olive oil, divided

1 clove garlic, halved

1 papaya, peeled, seeded, and chopped

4 plum tomatoes, finely chopped

½ small red onion, finely chopped

½ cup chopped fresh cilantro

1 teaspoon honey

½ teaspoon grated lemon peel

1. Preheat the oven to 450°F.

2. Brush the bread on both sides with 1 tablespoon of the oil. Place on a baking sheet and bake for 7 minutes, or until golden brown and crisp. Rub the toasted bread very lightly with the cut garlic clove.

3. In a medium bowl, combine the papaya, tomatoes, onion, cilantro, honey, lemon peel, and the remaining 1 tablespoon oil. Spoon on top of the toasted garlic bread.

makes 12 servings

per serving: 218 calories, 8 g protein, 42 g carbohydrates, 3 g fat, 0 g saturated fat, 3 g fiber, 424 mg sodium

pepper 'n smoke kale chips

prep time: 10 minutes • **total time:** 25 minutes

1. Preheat the oven to 350°F. Line 2 baking sheets with parchment paper.

2. Tear the kale into bite-size pieces. In a large bowl, toss the kale with the oil until evenly coated. Sprinkle with the paprika, salt, and pepper, tossing until coated.

3. Spread the kale in a single layer on the prepared baking sheets. Bake for 15 minutes, or until browned around the edges and crisped.

makes 4 servings

1	bunch (14 ounces) kale, ribs removed
1½	tablespoons extra-virgin olive oil
1	teaspoon smoked paprika
¼	teaspoon kosher salt
¼	teaspoon pepper

per serving: 76 calories, 3 g protein, 6 g carbohydrates, 6 g fat, 1 g saturated fat, 1 g fiber, 144 mg sodium

broccoli dip with multigrain chips

prep time: 10 minutes • **total time:** 40 minutes

1. Preheat the oven to 400°F. Coat 2 baking sheets with parchment paper.

2. Bring a large saucepan of lightly salted water to a boil over high heat. Add the broccoli, return to a boil, and cook for 3 minutes, or until bright green. Drain, rinse under cold water, and drain again. Pat the broccoli with paper towels to remove excess water. Finely chop.

3. Meanwhile, heat 2 tablespoons of the oil in a medium skillet over medium-high heat. Cook the onions and garlic for 5 minutes, stirring often, until the onions are softened. Remove from the heat and let cool for 10 minutes. Transfer to a bowl and stir in the broccoli, sour cream, mayonnaise, orange peel, salt, and pepper.

4. Arrange the tortilla wedges in a single layer on the prepared baking sheets and brush with the remaining 1 tablespoon of the oil. Bake for 5 minutes, or until lightly browned. Serve with the dip.

makes 12 servings

- 4 cups fresh broccoli florets
- 3 tablespoons extra-virgin olive oil, divided
- 2 onions, chopped
- 2 cloves garlic, minced
- ¾ cup light sour cream
- ½ cup olive oil mayonnaise
- 1 teaspoon grated orange peel
- ¾ teaspoon salt
- ⅛ teaspoon pepper
- 6 multigrain tortillas (7" to 8" diameter), cut into 8 wedges each

per serving: 149 calories, 4 g protein, 16 g carbohydrates, 9 g fat, 2 g saturated fat, 2 g fiber, 328 mg sodium

index

Boldface page references indicate photographs. Underscored references indicate boxed text, tables, or charts.